Manchild for Real

Ann Marie Edw[ards]

Hello, Brian,

Enjoy reading about Indiana's favorite rocker! Ain't that America.

Happy Birthday,

Dave

MANCHILD FOR REAL

The Life and Lyrics of
JOHN
COUGAR
MELLENCAMP

David Harshfield

David Harshfield

January 4, 1987

VANTAGE PRESS
New York / Washington / Atlanta
Los Angeles / Chicago

FIRST EDITION

All rights reserved, including the right of
reproduction in whole or in part in any form.

Copyright © 1986 by David Harshfield

Published by Vantage Press, Inc.
516 West 34th Street, New York, New York 10001

Manufactured in the United States of America
ISBN: 0-533-06647-6

Library of Congress Catalog Card No.: 85-90147

To Clara Mae Harshfield,
for her love
of writing;
to Mary, Anne, and Susan,
for their love;
to Harry Mellencamp,
for his spirit; and
to John Mellencamp,
for helping us
laugh at ourselves

CONTENTS

Acknowledgments ix

Chapter One.	Contradictions: Will the Real John Cougar Mellencamp Please Stand Up?	1
Chapter Two.	Romanticism versus Naturalism	8
Chapter Three.	Coming of Age	30
Chapter Four.	Sweet Success	44
Chapter Five.	The Guy I Hate	58
Chapter Six.	Son of Seymour	99
Chapter Seven.	*Chestnut Street Incident*	107
Chapter Eight.	*The Kid Inside*	113
Chapter Nine.	*A Biography*	125
Chapter Ten.	*John Cougar*	140
Chapter Eleven.	*Nothing Matters and What if It Did?*	148
Chapter Twelve.	*American Fool*	156
Chapter Thirteen.	*Uh-huh*	164
Chapter Fourteen.	*Scarecrow*	178
Chapter Fifteen.	Parting Comments	190

Notes 197
Bibliography 203

ACKNOWLEDGMENTS

The author expresses his sincere thanks and heartfelt gratitude to the following individuals who supplied information relevant to this biography: William W. Bailey, Brantley Blythe, Betty Bullard, Ritchie Clark, Patty Crane, Tim Day, Barbara Deboer, Avery Dittmer, Virginia Ernest, Judy Farris, Harry Knight, Bill Klaes, J. A. Mellencamp, Joe Mellencamp, Laura Mellencamp, Rose Mellencamp, Bryan Mundy, Julie Noblitte, Richard Pennybaker, Jim Plump, Elizabeth Rebber, Richard Reigel, Mark Ripley, Dave Shaw, Brett C. Sciarra, John W. Smith, Don Stover, and Herb Zumhingst. The author would also like to acknowledge the assistance of others who wish to remain anonymous. Without their aid, this book would not have been possible. Special thanks go to Cheryl Lewis for the typing and to Anne-Marie Edwards for the photographs.

Manchild for Real

Ann Marie Edwa

CHAPTER ONE

CONTRADICTIONS: WILL THE REAL JOHN COUGAR MELLENCAMP PLEASE STAND UP?

Christmas is a celebration of life, the birth of Christ. Christmas is a holiday for family love and for exchanging gifts that represent this undying love. Christmas is a season of Christian benevolence, human concern, bright decorations, and happy memories.

But for John Cougar Mellencamp, Christmas Day, 1983, was also a day of unrelenting loss. December 25, 1983, was the last day that John Mellencamp saw his grandfather alive. Harry "Speck" Mellencamp had been dying of cancer. Family members and close friends realized that the final day of reckoning was approaching. But this empty, shallow reality was not easy to bear. Because of the terminal nature of Grandfather Mellencamp's cancer, the hospital enjoined no rules concerning the number of visitors allowed in the room at any one time. Consequently, on a quiet Christmas afternoon, Harry Mellencamp's hospital room was filled with the relatives who respected him and revered him the most.

Harry Mellencamp had been a driving force in the lives of his own sons, as well as in the life of his grandson, known to the rock world as John Cougar, but known to Speck as John Mellencamp. Harry was a hard worker, a diligent individual and competitive spirit who expected others to achieve and to struggle and to endure. His grandson certainly did assimilate those lessons. But now Harry was lying on his deathbed, falling victim to a ravenous disease that even he could no longer combat.

This was the reality on December 25, 1983, when Harry's family gathered in his hospital room for what was to be their last gathering with Speck.

John Mellencamp moved next to Harry's bed. Here was the gentleman who encouraged and supported John throughout all the struggling years of striving to make his dream come true. Here was the gentleman who understood the importance of music in John's life, as well as appreciated the songwriting talent John possessed. Here was the gentleman who accepted the fact that John marched to a different drummer, that he was destined to do something other than farming or contracting. Here was the gentleman who believed in his grandson and who inspired his grandson's creative endeavors. Here was the gentleman whose death would mark a profound and deep loss.

Next to his grandfather's bed, John Mellencamp picked up his guitar, positioned himself comfortably close to his loving grandfather, and slowly began to sing very softly into his dying grandfather's ear. John sang "Silent Night" to his grandfather.

When John stopped singing, a dry eye was not to be found in the room. When John stopped singing, the spiritual essence of the Christmas season was present in that hospital room. When John stopped singing, one began to understand that a man's death is never for naught, that a man's life has meaning. After John stopped singing, the teary-eyed family realized that, in reality, they had gathered in Harry's room *not* because Harry was dying, but because Harry had lived and because Harry had loved and because Harry had touched their souls.

Later, after John's singing, Harry's wife, Laura Mellencamp, leaned toward her husband and asked, "Honey, did you know who that was?"

Fortunately, Harry was able to respond with, "Yes, that was John singing."

Perhaps there is a time to live and a time to die. Harry seemed to recognize that his time to die had arrived; his earthly release would soon arrive. A few hours after John sang "Silent Night" to him, around five o'clock Christmas afternoon, Harry Mellencamp slipped into a coma, from which he never returned. Harry "Speck" Mellencamp died about 5:30 on the morning of December 28, 1983. But the last music the gentleman ever heard was the comforting words of the familiar Christmas carol that his now-famous grandson sang into his ear just hours before his death.

Who is the man that the world has known as John Cougar, but who is striving so diligently and successfully to become known as John Cougar Mellencamp? Why are there so many contradictions and inconsistencies associated with this singer/songwriter? Don't we want to scream, "Will the real John Cougar Mellencamp please stand up?" Or, perhaps more to the point, don't we want to scream, "Will the media-hyped image of John Cougar please get off our backs?"

But, yes, John Cougar/John Mellencamp is a complex entanglement of diversity and contradiction. On one hand, he would have us believe him to be a reckless drinker, a rebellious snot, a foul-mouthed punk, and a macho stud. On the other hand, I have reason to believe that he is now a total abstainer from alcoholic beverages, that he possesses an intense loyalty to his family and friends, that he is a soft-spoken gentleman, and that he is a vulnerable, insecure person. On one hand, we are expected to believe that John is an aloof brat, a lackadaisical fool, an attention seeker, and a happy-go-lucky idiot. On the other hand, closer scrutiny shows us a sensitive person with a social awareness, as well as a man who is protecting his privacy amidst his recent fame while proving himself to be a respectable and responsible businessman in the process. How can all of these images be accurate? They are so contradictory. Why does John himself make statements that perpetuate the negative traits and make the favorable characteristics even harder to accept as fact?

John Cougar Mellencamp is, indeed, a maze of contradictory statements. Cracking jokes about his lustful youth, with his sexual abandon, John conceals the idea that today he is a devoted husband who is loyal to his wife. References to his beer-drinking, car-speeding days hide the image of a responsible, meticulous businessman running his multimillion-dollar operation. His hanging onto former friendships and his devotion to his relatives make it more difficult for his fans to comprehend his inner struggle to accept the new roles and responsibilities that arrived with success. The son who never understood his parents, nor thought that they understood him, is now the affectionate father of three admiring daughters. Does he work at fathering so he can reduce the distance between parent and child that existed during his own adolescence? The once-struggling artist who sought *any* public recognition is now an established star who guards and protects the privacy of his personal life. Does he still not feel as though he is totally established in the topsy-turvy field of rock entertainment, even though most others see this status as a given fact? His former feelings of inferiority are giving way to a flowering of self-acceptance. But this self-esteem and confidence generate fears and give rise to further doubts. Why did he divorce his first wife, a woman older than he, then remarry a woman younger than himself? Why does he continue to reside in the Bloomington/Seymour area, rather than relocate in Los Angeles or New York City? Does he feel more comfortable remaining close to his roots, in the Midwest? Is it easier and safer to be a big fish in a small stream rather than being a smaller fish in the large stream of the East or West? Does his devotion to former friends from his youth really show a disguised fear of the future? Is the rambunctious, macho image of his former years (alcohol, fists, and sex) now making it more frustrating for him to settle comfortably into his thirties and to be taken seriously? John has avoided falling into this popularized venue of androgenous rock star, but he is apparently grappling with a self-identity conducive to his adult status. The kid, after all, does grow up, even if he never gives in, as John himself is so quick to assert.

What makes John Cougar Mellencamp tick? What goes on inside the mental playground of this musical genius? What kind of a son is he? What type of a father is he? Was he a loyal husband to Priscilla, his first wife? Is he a loyal husband to Vicki, his present wife? Is money his motivating force? Or is the deep appreciation of music his compelling drive? To those who knew him before his fame, what kind of a person was he? How do some cousins and uncles see the now-famous rocker? How did these same relatives see him in the past? How do some close friends and former employers see him, both then and now? How do previous coaches and former teachers view him, as an athlete and/or as a student? How does the media image of John Cougar differ from the real person known as John Mellencamp? Does John today really have an inferiority complex, an identity crisis, and/or a distorted public image? Why does John seem to feed this negative public image, while at the same time attempting to devote more time to the quality of the music and less time to the hype of the image? Why does his hometown seem so unimpressed with the fact that a local boy has made a success of himself in such an intensely combative field? Has Seymour, Indiana, been negligent with her collective efforts at encouraging her native son?

John Cougar Mellencamp in concert projects an uncanny amount of charismatic energy. He sings, moves around the stage, emotes, jumps onto amplifiers, slides down ladders, dances insatiably, and even jumps upon the shoulders of fellow bandsmen. This electrifying energy seems to be nonstop, reflecting his commitment to his music, his joy at publicly performing, and his devotion to his loyal fans. John wants to conclude the concert with a feeling that he has given the spectators their money's worth, that he has solidified his reputation as a capable rocker, and that he is an honest performer who need not pull magic tricks out of a bag. At that proverbial bottom line, John's admirable sixth sense tells him that those fans are out there to see him in concert. This realization is not pure egotism, as it is essentially a valid deduction for him to make. Therefore, his responsibility is to uphold this respect and admiration from his fans by arranging and presenting a solid show, based upon the true spirit of rock and roll and the talents of John Cougar Mellencamp. This, indeed, is what John attempts to do and what John succeeds at doing. What more can fans expect?

All of us play various roles; this is part of life. At home, in a pastoral environment, we are spouses, parents, confidantes, and lovers. At work, in a more perplexing setting, we are directors, bosses, organizers, and promoters. At church, we are reflective and forgiving. On a ball field, we are aggressive and determined. At times, these diverse roles become intermingled. Logic tells us, however, that John Cougar Mellencamp is entitled to the same role-playing extravaganza that we delightfully call the game of life.

Perhaps Mr. Mellencamp looks dubiously over his shoulder to a simpler time, but his catapult to success in 1982 has certainly shown him to be an avid believer and a sincere devotee of the American dream. This book, perhaps, is about that American dream. This book is about a man named John Jay Mellencamp, who, at the beginning of a recording career, found himself rechristened Johnny Cougar. Perhaps his anger at this name change has been delved into too much, but whether this exploratory venture was shrewd or foolhardy, one fact remains unquestioned: John Cougar Mellencamp finally proved successful in his authentic climb to the top. He has delighted many, outraged some, and amused others. But, as he concentrates both on his destination *and* on the quality of his ascent, he is taking hold of the reins himself, accepting the accolades or the disgrace from whatever decision he makes. To some, he is a vulgar, childish kid, overly dependent upon projecting a strong, macho appeal. To others, he is a heroic figure who has never deflected from his obsessive desire to break into the lucrative and creative world of rock stardom.

Even though he laughingly mocks the American dream, John is the very essence of this dream. John is intelligent, wise, and perceptive. He is also a pragmatist who at times attempts to shock us with his vulgarity and/or rage. On certain occasions, he seems to be still out to get even with somebody or to prove something to somebody. But John Cougar Mellencamp is a complex set of contradictions, both inside and out, as he sets the cadence to which he will march. Aggravating at times? Of course! But we all respect this brand of confidence and moxie; it is indigenous to our beloved concept of the American dream. And John Cougar Mellencamp embodies that concept; indeed, he reenforces our conviction that the dream lives and that the dream still works. Harry Mellencamp, the loving and supportive grandfather who died on December 28, 1983, was, indeed, a fortunate man. Harry was able to see his grandson become famous; but more important than that, Harry Mellencamp, born of a different age, in November of 1903, witnessed a rebirth of the American dream. His witnessing such a revelation in the personified form of his own beloved grandson was, indeed, a tribute to all the values of God, country, and family that we Americans cherish so dearly.

CHAPTER TWO

ROMANTICISM VERSUS NATURALISM

John Cougar Mellencamp became a household word, so to speak, in 1982, with the colossal success of two hit singles that earned him two Grammy Awards. "Jack and Diane" and "Hurts So Good" skyrocketed him from being a hitherto obscure young man from Seymour, Indiana, to being a definitive force in pop music—a talent to be reckoned with, a personality to be acknowledged.

Today, in various interviews, both in print and over the media, John Cougar Mellencamp seems somewhat embarrassed by the sophomoric nature of these two songs. He is gratified at the public's appreciation of them. After all, this acceptance culminated his decade-long struggle to become a recognized artist in a highly competitive field. Yet, in retrospect, Mellencamp seems frustrated over the public's concept of what "Jack and Diane" means. On "Good Morning America," in an interview shown Monday, April 23, 1984, Ms. Joan Lunden asked John about the meaning of holding onto "sixteen." Smiling, John responded by saying that the now-famous words have been misinterpreted. According to Mellencamp, the idea that he wanted to convey was that we should hang onto whatever age we liked best. If age sixteen was that age, then we should hang onto age sixteen. However, John said he was pleased with sixteen, but also with eighteen, twenty, and twenty-seven. He is apparently a happy person who has reaped the most out of life at whatever age he was.

But, in context, has the public misinterpreted the line? Or has the writer altered his preception of what he would like the song to be? In another interview, John pokes fun at the concept that life goes on, even when the excitement and the fun are gone. Deceptively simplistic lines like this one are the kind we can all relate to. All of us, as a matter of coping with and surviving in this game of life, have experienced depression—that low that forces us to ponder the meaning of life and the importance of existence. Indeed, studies reveal that suicides are most likely to occur between the ages of eighteen and twenty-five. Indeed, life's thrills must be drained from many of us. But in this interview, John related an incident when a man told him that he whispered those lines to his wife, whose father had died. The wife felt some comfort from the human warmth and simple meaning of the line. With a chuckle, Mellencamp says the line was not supposed to mean that, yet he felt good, nevertheless, that the line was able to alleviate the suffering of this woman whose father had died.[1]

The artist apparently strives to write songs that convey empathy and feelings that are shared by all of us, the human community. This author wonders if John Cougar Mellencamp is overly critical of himself when he demeans the impact of the famous, memorable line from "Jack and Diane." Any artist is undoubtedly flattered at the success of his creative impulses, but then an artist sometimes finds himself, in retrospect, having to go back and interpret his own work. Instead of downplaying the sophomoric quality of the song, we should recognize the song for what it is: a love song about two teens who are trying to understand their own roles in society while at the same time coming to terms with their own sensuality and their own love for each other.

Let's accept this line about life going on for what it is: a simple, but heartfelt expression of frustration shared between a boy and a girl. Let's not feel obligated to make apologies for the song; also, let's not attempt, as this writer thinks John Cougar Mellencamp himself was attempting to on "Good Morning America," to remove the line from its context and alter its significance. I do not understand how John Cougar Mellencamp can say he was meaning to tell us that we should hang onto whatever age we felt best. He might personally believe this, but this is not what he was telling us to do in his poignantly touching song about two young lovers. The age sixteen is specifically mentioned as the age to hang onto, since age forces us to become men and women all too quickly, changing everything.

As a fan, I admire Cougar's ability to make us feel positive about ourselves, but I think Mellencamp is a bit confused here himself. Jack and Diane need to hang onto sixteen; age sixteen is also the age in many states where we become able to get a driver's license, which makes age sixteen a definitive age for carrying us over the threshold of maturity. Like John, I agree that we should all strive for that elusive happiness. But John must not lose sight of the tremendous impact that the lyrics of "Jack and Diane" had on its teenage audience. Jack and Diane had dreams—collectively and individually. All of us do. When they saw these dreams threatened or, worse, crumbling down before their eyes, they became scared and immobile. They needed each other, but their best was not good enough.

Once again, with "Hurts So Good," Mellencamp has managed to hang a catchy title onto a song that appeals to people of almost any age. As the melody begins, the singer says that, as he ages, he must discard his youthful ideas. As a youngster, he says, he wanted to escape from the reality of being a kid. But now, older and burdened with responsibility, he yearns for those carefree days. We have all experienced the fear and the agony of growing up. Regardless of financial background, social heritage, mental ability, or of any other factor, each and every individual has felt the pressures to grow up, to mature, to be accepted as an adult, on equal footing with others. The irony is that, even though this maturation process is a threatening, challenging ordeal, it is a turn of events—an initiation—that each individual wants to encounter, because the rewards of growing up and being adult far outweight the scant looks directed toward one who never tries or never succeeds.

"Hurts So Good" is really, then, about initiation, about sex, and about pressures. John Cougar Mellencamp has harnessed his creative energy into composing another song that might be somewhat sophomoric in its lyrics, but manages to strike at a communal human desire that we all possess. Like Jack and Diane, the young protagonists in "Hurts So Good" are about to cross a threshold of initiation. This is a frightening thought, yet the resulting knowledge form this initiation will make them stronger individuals, now more able to be at peace with their own sexual feelings. Think about your first sexual experience. Remember the fears: *Will we be caught? If so, what punishment and shame will be brought to bear upon us? Will this encounter be at all painful [particularly for the girl]? Will my sexual apparatus function properly? Will my performance be satisfactory? Will pregnancy be the result? Will the ecstasy be as intense as everybody leads us to believe? Should we experiment with oral sex first? At least pregnancy will be avoided then. Afterwards, will we still be able to be friends, or will the reality of the sexual intercourse place too much emotional and psychological strain on our unstable feelings for each other? How guilty will we feel? Will the guilt subside or will it endure forever?*

Questions such as these pretty much bring the memories of our first sexual encounter home to roost. The protagonists in Mellencamp's Grammy-winning song jump through the burning hoops on all of these questions, as we all did at one time or another or will sometime in the future. But, as usual, the lovers' parents do not discover what has occurred, thus they escape any direct punishment. Whatever pain existed was certainly tolerable, and all seemed to be fine: erection and lubrication occurred; the ecstasy was there, but perhaps overrated; and the puritanical guilt feelings ultimately diminished. This couple endured and confronted all of these pressures—including the pressure to enter into the sensually heightened, pregnancy-free indulgence of oral sex.

The unnamed lovers in this haunting melody are similar to

Jack and Diane. They have dreams and goals, yet they also deal with pressures and desires. They are so real—and so like us—that the result is an uneasiness that allows us to like and to identify with them: to understand their fears, to sympathize with the discomfort of their pressures, and to delight in their increased wisdom. To me, John Cougar Mellencamp shows tremendous insight and laudable depth with these songs, which are not as sophomoric as they appear. He should not be discrediting the depth or the impact of either. Both are human songs, not idea songs.

The summer of 1983—July, to be exact—at a sixteen day blowout at the Shack (a recording studio)—the next batch of songs from John Cougar Mellencamp was born. The *Uh-huh* album, released in the fall of 1983, has a cover that uses John's legal surname—Mellencamp—coupled with the sexier, more commercial name hung around Mellencamp's neck like an albatross by his first manager, Tony DeFries. With "John Cougar Mellencamp" written at head level, to his left, John is surrounded by two angels on each side of him. But, beware, cautions the star: the angels have horns.

Uh-huh begins with the successful "Crumblin' Down." Picturing himself as the whipping boy, the victim of people who are no good because they cannot be trusted or loved, Cougar mesmerizes us with a comfortable blend of hostility and tolerance. Denying he was ever a sinner, he defends the elusive, unnamed "crime" of the song by saying he has only learned to bend the rules in order to have his own way. But some of these people are waiting for him to fall, so they can "claim my crumblin' walls." Any artist has critics; any successful performer has made enemies. Exactly who these folks are who want him to fail, to suffer utter defeat, then to come "crumblin' down" is open to a witch hunt of speculation.

But it seems as though the artist is not trying to convey bitterness or hostility, even though the rage within exists in a real sense. What Mellencamp seems to be attempting is to project a sense of tolerance and mutual acceptance amidst the differences of opinions. The lyrics continue, admonishing the listener with the audacious charge that he is obnoxious, lazy, and uneducated. Yet Cougar looks at his strengths: being a good dancer; knowing where he is headed; and acknowledging the trouble that he realizes he is to people, apparently even to those he loves and cares about and who love and care about him. And with all this, he possesses the human need to have a lover who caresses him and breathes into his ear.

The speaker of these words is not a totality unto himself. The speaker acknowledges that he has caused problems and that he has enemies. Yet he is striving for some stability in his existence, so as to diminish the odds of his walls tumblin', crumblin' down. All this speaker seems to want is somebody who will treat him the same, in spite of his pictures appearing in the paper. This sounds autobiographical—as though Cougar was talking about himself.

What is the meaning of the title of the song? What, exactly, is supposed to come crumbling down? Or, perhaps more to the point, what does the speaker want to come crumbling down? Or, does the speaker fear that something will come crumblin' down, leaving him overly vulnerable?

As a frustrated young musician, struggling for recognition in a highly competitive field, Mellencamp endured many hard lessons: he lost money given to promotors, sacrificed his ego with the forced name change, and lost self-esteem with the various rejections from record-company experts who said he had no talent. Most of us can understand, then, that under such circumstances environmental determinism would force a person to develop a hardened outer crust, to adopt a subsurface tendency to keep a stiff upper lip, to fancy himself as an underdog. Our psychological defense mechanisms seem to cut in for us so as to assure us our survival.

I wish I could have known young John Mellencamp ten years ago, as a young twenty-four-year-old bravely venturing from his small hometown into the fast lane of rock music, in the cold, big city; or I wish I could have known him twenty years ago, as a fourteen-year-old growing up and, as he would have us believe, anyway—drinking and fighting his way through junior and senior high school; or I wish I could have known him thirty years ago, as a four-year-old with few worries or cares. Knowing him then would have allowed me to become a part of his life during the so-called early years and see him mature. But the key years here, perhaps, are the teen years. Was he really the drinker and the fighter who, along with his rough cohorts, was out for a fun time and a good lay? Or did this image emanate from the bitterness of the world that he saw later, when he left Seymour? Or was this image a sloppily executed media hype to promote an unknown rocker into the public spotlight?

When I first heard John say he was from a small town in Indiana, I figured he meant a town of less than 1,000 inhabitants. I hail from Fremont, Michigan, with a population of under 5,000, yet Fremont is the largest town in Newaygo County and was, when I was there, the only town in the county with a stoplight. And Fremont only had one! Yes, the concept of small is relative, as we all know. Nevertheless, I was amazed to learn that Seymour, Indiana, is the hometown of more than 17,000 people. This makes Seymour, Indiana, about the same size as Flushing, Michigan, where I now reside. Although Flushing is small compared to Flint or Detroit, it is not the stereotyped small city, nor is it small compared to the many bergs located nearby. Look on an Indiana map: Seymour is in darker print than many smaller towns around her.

In any event, John thinks he is from a small town. John also thinks he was a roughneck while growing up in Seymour. Maybe he was, but what was considered rough in Seymour might have been considered child's play in Indianapolis or in Detroit.

To those who see "Crumblin' Down" as a happy, energetic, optimistic song, as I do, we can speculate here. Perhaps the singer/writer—Mellencamp himself—is sending his audience of fans a message that he would like to see this wall of macho vulnerability tumble into ruin. Perhaps the singer/writer—Mellencamp himself, remember—is challenging his audience of fans to let him begin anew, to project a different image, to be like he was before he did and said many of the things he now regrets, as he was climbing over the roadblocks on his way to stardom. Perhaps Mellencamp is asserting a new image, one he sees as more honest, one he sees as the real him. Like I said, I wish I knew him during his teen years in Seymour. But during the sixties and the seventies, how rough and violent a "gang" would a town like Seymour, Indiana, tolerate?

To me, the symbolic wall that crumbles to ruin is the hardened shell that circumstances built around John. This "joke of the industry" ruffled feathers and created enemies. The "macho teen" in Seymour apparently did likewise. But now, in 1986, neither of these name tags seems to fit. Seymour's hero still lives close to home, loving the people and the life-style. The rock star has proven to himself and to the industry that he is a viable force, a popular entertainer, and an adequate talent. He deserves and has received considerable respect.

Witness the lyrics of one of the less popular songs on the same *Uh-huh* album: "Golden Gates." No video was made for this number, which Mellencamp claims describes vividly the way he feels. Here is a man who struggled and fought for about seven years before winning, in 1982, significant recognition for his creative genius. In "Golden Gates," Mellencamp admonishes his listeners with the warning that golden gates will not open wide, that streets will not be paved in pearl, and that angels will not sing with harps. The real world—characterized by uncertain futures and by bosses who negotiate tremendous deals without recognizing the importance of the little guy—is tough and competitive. This realistic determinism drives the speaker (John) to seek escape and solace by retreating to a private sanctuary (a big suite) overlooking the park. There, alone with his trusted lover, he can communicate the only truths that matter: the promises that come from the heart. The street-wise Mellencamp really searches for comfort and understanding, not confrontation and division. Yet, to admit these feelings is to become vulnerable, to discard the pseudo-macho front.

Symbolically, the golden gates represent the attainment of some goal. In Cougar's case, the golden gates that wouldn't open without his traveling the rough, bumpy road to success must be the recognition he has so painstakingly and diligently sought. The world we know is one where we are pretty much on our own, to fight our own battles, to dream our own dreams, to make our own mistakes, and to enjoy our own triumphs. Logic would indicate that the masters with their big deals going on might be the record company itself—complete with producers, promotors, critics, and so on. But, in a mellow mood, what the singer/writer—again, I suspect John Cougar Mellencamp himself—wants is a source of permanence and beauty (the suite overlooking the park), plus a trusting and understanding person with whom to share it.

To Mellencamp, in "Golden Gates," truth—that elusive monster—comes from the heart. This sounds romantic, characteristic of American poets between 1820 and 1860. Isn't the history of mankind really a search for truth? Doesn't each individual find himself/herself questioning the world as it is given to him/her: God and the church, school and the teachers, government and the politicians, friends and the family. Whether intentionally or not, Mellencamp has composed another song that hits at the basic communal heartbeat of our individualism. Truth becomes equated with sincerity, warmth, honesty, and other such emotions that we westerners associate with the heart.

In this song, Mellencamp lets his listener know that he has witnessed too much loneliness and suffering already, that he does not want to see another lonely man or another woman crying for a savior as he or she hangs onto a moneyman's hand. This implies a prostitute/pimp relationship, once the prostitute begins to yearn for escape through a redemptive savior. Symbolically, we have another understanding, trusting person—in this case, a father substitute, perhaps—but still a person who fills a basic void that all of us experience in our lives. Mellencamp says we will have to take care of ourselves, yet he expresses an inner fear that doubts whether he possesses all the strength he requires to live the way he wants. All of us would no doubt relish the fame and acclaim that has befallen John Cougar Mellencamp over the past several years. Yet fame and success do cause adjustments in one's life-style and do necessitate the gearing up of an inner strength to cope with the accolades and the responsibilities.

Because I enjoy both the lyrics and the melody of "Golden Gates," I have listened to it frequently. More than any other song he has written and released to the public, "Golden Gates" presents John Cougar Mellencamp as a Stephen Crane type of naturalist who knows that the world would be a more calming place within which to live if the Edgar Allen Poe type of romanticism were correct.

Like John Cougar Mellencamp, naturalists believe that reality is a struggle; that success requires a struggle, yet does not guarantee either contentment or happiness; that the world owes us nothing; that we are on our own, to fail or to succeed; and that the environment (nature or man) might thwart our dreams. Stephen Crane always comes to my mind whenever I think of American naturalism as it surfaces in poetry.

Stephen Crane wrote two poems that are short, but powerful, statements of his naturalism. "Golden Gates" reminds me of both of these poems: similar symbolism, similar themes.

A Man Said to the Universe

A man said to the universe:
"Sir, I exist!"
"However," replied the universe,
"The fact has not created in me
A sense of obligation."
                                        1899

A Man Saw a Ball of Gold in the Sky

A man saw a ball of gold in the sky;
He climbed for it,
And eventually he achieved it—
It was clay.

Now this is the strange part;
When the man went to the earth
And looked again,

> Lo, there was the ball of gold.
> Now this is the strange part:
> It was a ball of gold.
> Ay, by the heavens, it was a ball of gold.
>
> 1895

    If Stephen Crane were alive today and if he were to ever meet John Cougar Mellencamp, my hunch is that they would be pretty close friends. They think alike. But I also suspect that John Cougar Mellencamp could have been a pretty close friend with Edgar Allan Poe, who died in 1849, a penniless alcoholic and drug addict. The bond that would unite them is not Poe's financial state nor his personal habits. The binding force that would unite them is their quest to find beauty, truth, and understanding. Poe's tragic, short life in no way parallels the life of John Cougar Mellencamp, but the haunting nature of Poe's writing, along with his vulnerable openness, remind me of a haunting and vulnerable John Cougar Mellencamp, as he portrays himself in "Golden Gates." We are all vulnerable, however; we should never forget this fact. We should also applaud a poet—of the past, present, or future—who possesses the raw courage to admit he or she is a weak, uncertain, fearful individual who needs some strength, like promises from the heart, to help him or her endure and prevail.

    Some will see a comparison of a contemporary rock star to such greats as Poe and Crane as ludicrous and foolish. Yet any creative mind will be compared and contrasted to other creative minds. Comparison and contrast are our methods of intellectually sorting details; these processes enhance our understanding. Poe, a troubled man, was a creative genius. Crane had problems, too, yet his creative genius was allowed to emerge and to blossom. Many believe that John Cougar Mellencamp is a troubled person, because of his alleged brashness, vulgarity, egotism, and impatience. The process of living necessitates our coping with problems. But the beauty of this process comes to life when we see the creative genius burst forth into public view and into public acceptance.

Ironically, coincidence has Edgar Allan Poe and John Cougar Mellencamp sharing the same birthday, October 7—1809 and 1951, respectively. If videos were around in Poe's day, I'd wager that he would have made one of "Annabel Lee." I think John Cougar Mellencamp has made a mistake not to market a video of "Golden Gates." The increasingly large audience of fans who enjoy Cougar's work would witness a different John Cougar Mellencamp: mellow, vulnerable, and insecure, yet also contemplative, honest, and sensitive. My guess is that John Cougar Mellencamp will continue to grow in popularity. Besides meaning more profits flowing into the till, this popularity also propels an artist into a new brand of creativity. This new brand could take the form of a mere commercial sellout to his fans. But John Cougar Mellencamp is not so interested in commercialism. Mellencamp's new brand of creativity will project a somewhat more serious writer who will try to be more precise in delivering his message, but will also be more open and vulnerable to his loyal fans. Vulnerability is not as much of a threat when it is harnessed with public support and private confidence.

Hats off to Edgar Allan Poe. Hats off to Stephen Crane. Hats off to John Cougar Mellencamp. Three romantics; three naturalists; three thinkers—all sought or are seeking basic human needs and expressed or are expressing this search through the written word. Writers, though, must combat their impulsive instinct at times, since a creative person—in order to be understood and appreciated—must sometimes sublimate his or her true feelings by burying them in a morass of abstract, vague verbiage that conveys little if any meaning to the reader/listener. Luckily, Poe, Crane, and Mellencamp successfully merge this comfortable blend of romanticism and naturalism. Their written word manages to make us feel like we are not as far off-course as we sometimes think. We empathize with them and understand ourselves more completely in the process.

As John Cougar Mellencamp grows older, as we all do,

perhaps he will feel more comfortable with promoting the songs that seem to be made in his heart. Courage and confidence are needed for an individual to confess his or her inner feelings. Time and success frequently prove to be the womb within which this courage and confidence can incubate and hatch.

Success is growing for John Cougar Mellencamp, so this is a positive sign that these further changes will become reality. If Mellencamp really feels that the lyrics of "Golden Gates" are personally meaningful to him, why does he regress and make a video out of "Authority Song" rather than out of "Golden Gates?" No doubt, "Authority Song" proved to be a commercially successful video and song—it has a natural appeal to adolescents who see themselves as fighting authority. And, as in reality, Mellencamp concedes that authority always wins. So he just grins. "Authority Song," in my opinion, is not indicative of John Cougar Mellencamp at his best. On the other hand, any song with the Mellencamp signature and any video featuring John Cougar Mellencamp will be a commercial success and a musical hit.

When interviewed on MTV, Mellencamp stated that the original idea for the "Authority Song" video was to splice in tapes depicting people who had taken a courageous stand to fight authority. Some of these people would have been historical figures and others would be more contemporary heroes, from what the singer said in the interview. But the problem, Mellencamp continued, smiling in frustration, was that there were so many types to select from that the magnitude of the chore became overwhelming and the original idea was abandoned. Mellencamp's honesty here is admirable; hearing about the original idea for the video undoubtedly makes many of us think that it would have resulted in a superior finished product. The video then would have conveyed a sense of historical relevance, an aura of timeless universality, and a clarification of the song's real concept of authority. With the originial concept, the authority being challenged would be fought for a purpose, a principle. With the actual video, this laudable concept becomes misplaced and lost.

Why, then, was the video of "Authority Song" so popular? As previously stated, one reason is because the songwriter and chief performer is the popular star. Almost anything he produces will receive media attention, public acclaim and popularity. More importantly, in my opinion, though, the popularity of the "Authority Song" video and of the song itself is due largely to some instinctual ability of Cougar to hit at the essential heartstring that makes us all human. All of us feel that we fight authority and that we generally lose. How frequently do we hear people say, "You can't fight City Hall"? Our colloquial language is full of cute phrases that imply that we cannot confront some bureaucratic entity and be heard.

Cougar's opening lines overwhelm the listener with their directness. Forcing us into an uncomfortable, compromising position, smirking at us in the process, an unidentified "they" define themselves as the victor. But Mellencamp thinks that such treatment of another person is a complete and total disgrace, as the victim loses his confidence, his dignity, and his self-esteem.

What individual cannot personally identify with being in that position? The "they"—the symbolic authority figure—might be a parent, teacher, police officer, or any other adult in a position of authority. The speaker in the poem even says he goes to the preacher—another symbol of authority—for advice and for the strength to continue the fight. The preacher tells him to grow up, to forget about being strong and macho. Probably the preacher didn't use the double negative that Mellencamp used, but the grammatical oversight fits into the beat of the line. And, what individual hasn't been told, "Grow up; act your age"? Isn't this what the preacher really retorted to our victimized protagonist? And haven't we all seen growing up in terms of approaching death? The hero of our song says that he worries about old age because he worries about dying. He loves life too much to consider death. Mellencamp doesn't like to preach to folks, but when I first heard this song, I found this idea comforting. Many adolescents contemplate suicide because they are unable to cope with the frustration of life and to understand the finality of death. Here, however, is a popular singer saying that death is not something he wants. Fighting authority and losing is better than dying—a prolife position even in the midst of great odds. This "campish" theme from Mellencamp is refreshing and comforting: life is worth living, so we must prevail!

In this respect, rock stars become heroic leaders in the eyes of fans. Leadership is a unique art unto itself, as it requires both force and vision—two traits of poetic skill, I believe. In Greek mythology, Apollo provided Cassandra with the gift of prophecy. But then Apollo turned the gift into a curse by causing all who heard Cassandra's warnings to disbelieve them. All of us, at one time or another, feel like Cassandra. The speaker in "Authority Song" must feel like her—always confronting authority, but always losing because the authority figure won't listen to an opposing or a differing viewpoint. The opinions and visions of the speaker are never taken seriously, frequently forcing the protagonist to throw in the towel and bow to adversity. But leaders love life.

"Authority Song," though, needs one more verse, especially in view of the decision to drop the original concept for the video. I enjoyed the symbolism of the existing video. The various figures of authority (domestic, social, occupational, military) sit around a boxing ring watching the speaker fight his battle. Even the roped ring becomes a symbolic representation of being closed in, imposed upon, deprived of freedom, forced into total capitulation. This symbolism is both clever and functional, as it does serve to reinforce the meaning of the song. But one more verse could clarify the image of fighting authority in much the same way that the original idea for doing the video would have done. The original idea of having film clips of people confronting authority would allow Mellencamp to clarify and narrow the scope of fighting. Charles de Gaulle once said, "Nothing more enhances authority than silence." Yet this silence, he warned, must appear to conceal strength and determination. Leadership must be courted like a woman, we are told. A French proverb offers a worthy prescription that applies here: "Pursue the woman and she will flee; retreat and she will follow." An additional verse—or the original video concept—could have gone a step further, showing us that defiance and hostility and confrontation are not the only methods by which we can deal with authority. John Cougar Mellencamp himself knows this, no doubt, yet for some reason curtailed his song without letting us know he is aware of it. Once we learn to fight authority with silence (strength plus determination), we will know how to win some (not all) battles. But we can do more than be grinning losers who may or may not have made a point. All authority is not evil, yet some authority needs bottling. John Cougar Mellencamp, at his best, owes it to his fans to go this extra mile—to add that extra depth and insight to a song with an already keen concept.

What really makes young Mr. Mellencamp tick? Study the *Uh-huh* album. Mellencamp tells us that he is pleased with the album. No doubt, he has commercially profited, because the album has gone double platinum, meaning it has sold around 2 million copies. Actually, it has sold nearly 3 million copies. Any artist would be gratified that the public was so openly appreciative of his or her endeavors. And what better way is there for the public to display this open acceptance than to purchase a product? In all fairness, however, money itself—the accumulation of vast wealth—does not seem to turn John Mellencamp on. So what does keep his creative juices flowing? What makes John Mellencamp tick?

Self-expression, emoting, is what makes John Mellencamp tick. At the same time, he seems reluctant to come out and declare this to be a fact. True, he says that "John Cougar" was just a game he played. Yet as an adolescent struggling for his niche in the power structure of peer rivalries in Seymour, Indiana, John Mellencamp was apparently a game also. Now, as a thirty-four–year–old looking back and as a successful rock star looking forward, John Mellencamp is doing what we all do: getting in contact with himself so he knows what is going on. This task is not easy.

Three videos have been made from songs that appeard on the successful *Uh-huh* album. The first, "Crumblin' Down," propels a sense of frustrated, thwarted hostility at the reader. True, because the performer is John Cougar Mellencamp, we listen to and enjoy the video, yet we do not really learn anything concrete from the video. Unless we analyze the video on our own and speculate on its meaning, we do not see that a great deal of thought went into the song. In the third video, "Authority Song," we see, once again, a person who seems to be trapped and victimized by the "system," but we also relate to a person who has not yet learned how to handle the authority figures in his life. We feel a bit of sympathy and are able to relate his feelings of defeat (since authority always wins) to our own desperate, unfulfilled lives. But, as with "Crumblin' Down," we do not manage to learn anything specific. The second video is based on "Pink Houses." This, in my opinion, is the best of the three videos, because it is the best of the three songs. My question, implied before, is why the oversight? Why was there no video of "Golden Gates"?

But "Pink Houses" comes considerably closer to expressing the real John Mellencamp than either the "Crumblin' Down" video or the "Authority Song" video. John seems to be moved and influenced by simple values that are basic to all of us, as human beings. Although sophomoric at times, his biggest hits seem to reflect this reality. To some extent, Mellencamp himself shares this opinion of "Pink Houses." He says:

> I think this is the best song I've ever written. I was driving back from the Indianapolis airport with a friend on a highway elevated forty feet over the ground, and looked down to see an old guy sitting in his backyard in front of a pink house with a dog in his arms staring up at me with this real contented smile on his face. It was obvious that he thought he'd really made it in life. But there he was with a damned six-lane highway running through his backyard![2]

The initial lyrics of "Pink Houses" describe this scene: the black man with an interstate running through his yard. Why do you suppose John changed the dog he describes in the real observation of the scene to the cat that he actually uses in the words to the song? Anyway, this man thinks he has the world by the tail, even though an interstate runs through his front yard.

John Mellencamp seems to emote genuine concern and sorrow for this man—a man who has been passed over by life, a man who has learned to accept what comes his way and to make the best of it, rather than determine his own destiny. In another verse, John Mellencamp emotes sincere sympathy for the young man in a T-shirt who listens to his rock station, wondering where all of his dreams went. I wonder if John Mellencamp sometimes wonders if he is going to pinch himself, wake up from the dream, and find himself working for the phone company again. Finally, in the last verse, John Mellencamp again projects a poignant understanding of the way life works. Many people exist by their high-rise jobs and endure with their Gulf of Mexico vacations. But identifying the winners and the losers doesn't really matter, according to the lyrics, because, in the long run, it's the simple man—perhaps the middle class—that pays the bill for the thrills and the pills that kill. Perhaps Mellencamp has lost me here, with his specific point, but he hasn't lost me when it comes to grasping his basic love for and understanding of the simple, basic human feelings that we all encounter as we live, enjoy, and endure our daily existence. John Cougar Mellencamp is a feeling, sensitive individual, even though he sometimes shudders at revealing these traits.

But, from the heart, John Mellencamp loves small towns, people who are passed over by the bulldozer of life, and America. The mere fact that John Mellencamp continues to reside in the Seymour, Indiana, area, outside Bloomington, is a testament to the fact that he loves Seymour and its surrounding areas. This love serves as a salute to small towns and to the values and traditions they nurture. Looking beyond his origins, though, Mellencamp shows us that Seymour showed him how to love people, also. Some people are easy to care about, because they are so perfect and wonderful. But the folks Mellencamp cares about are not always so perfect, not always so wonderful. Mellencamp, in many ways, loves, understands, and perpetuates what America symbolizes. Mellencamp is strong on symbolism. The black man with the interstate, the young greaser with the lost dreams, and the winners and the losers who live out their lives—Mellencamp only tells us about them, without passing judgment. This is the personification of the melting-pot image of America: the nonjudgmental, open-armed, ever empathic man who strives to coexist in a symbiotic relationship with all people—not just those who are easy to love and appreciate.

This symbolic split between fantasy and reality is a problem for all of us, not just John Mellencamp, from Seymour, Indiana. Fantasy worlds allow us to escape into our dreams. Life, there, becomes unique, pleasant, and totally under our control. As children, we crawl around barking like dogs, slither around hissing like snakes, and run around buzzing like bees. Pretending we are a member of a lower species excites our creativity. As we enter childhood, we climb ladders with fire fighters, chase robbers with the police officers, and explore planets with astronauts. Our fantasy worlds have left the animal kingdom and become a smidgeon closer to reality. Then, like a downed 747, adolescence crashes down upon us. Any semblance of reality disappears from our fantasy world again, as we become aspiring movie stars, affluent jet-setters, and controversial rock performers. Some would say, in fact, that with the latter at least, reality not only had departed, but the fantasy had regressed into the animal world again, as our infant fantasies did. True, we realize all along that our chances of becoming an actor or an actress, jet-setter, or rock star are almost nil. But the dream lives, the escape comforts, and the fantasty endures. But for John Cougar Mellencamp, the fantasy did more than merely endure. For him, the fantasy blossomed into his reality.

Like young Mellencamp, many teenagers form bands, dreaming of the fame and fortune associated with stardom. The adults hate to destroy this hope, yet are reluctant to encourage such aspirations, knowing that the chances of success are so limited. Around 1956, while in the sixth grade, I became a rocker when Elvis Presley became the newly discovered talent sensation. Many adolescents dreamed about the fame and fortune of stardom, dreamed about traveling and singing while on tour, and dreamed about the thrill and excitement of being the center of attention. Our psyches were adequately indulged with these dreams, as we really knew we would probably never become famous like Elvis Presley or like any of the other performing rock artists. But the dreams provided us with a fantasized escape, a psychological pressure valve. Elvis Presley belonged to us, not to our parents. Elvis was a symbol of youth, the future. In contrast, the president of the United States, the grandfatherly Dwight David Eisenhower, was a symbol of age, the past. Or so we seemed to define and to classify these two famous individuals. Nevertheless, symbolic conflicts developed here, as the adults were aghast at Elvis, refusing to accept him, while the teenagers and adolescents were not attuned to Eisenhower. We believed in Elvis and what he represented. We believed in Elvis's future; too bad the dream died on August 16, 1977.

But the point is that only part of our interest in rock performers is their music and their talent. Another element of our interest in them hinges upon their behavior and their personality. What teenager today has not heard about the controversy surrounding Elvis's first appearance on "The Ed Sullivan Show" in 1956, the same year John Mellencamp entered this world? The gyrating hips were not televised, even though Elvis professed to be a God-fearing boy who loved his parents, his country, and his church. Nevertheless, Elvis was photographed for the television appearance only from the waist up. His claim that the gyrating hips were another manifestation of his musical expression was ignored; his dancing was not deemed acceptable for a family-oriented, prime-time, Sunday-evening telecast.

Controversy, it seems, has always surrounded rock stars—before Elvis and after Elvis. Look at their life-styles—flashy, wasteful, overindulgent, flamboyant, irresponsible, and reckless. Look at their careers—financially lucrative, generally short, and wearily tedious. These stars are apt to reside in New York City or on the West Coast, in California. These stars are apt to make public remarks that are not always complimentary to their peers. These stars are apt to squander large sums of money in order to indulge in a life of alcohol, other drugs, and sex. These stars frequently die relatively young. Living fast, they leave attractive corpses. Did the money descend upon these young talents at too early an age for them to handle the responsibility? Did the glory and the notoriety arrive too easily to be genuinely appreciated and nurtured? Did the fame and the public adoration extinguish the real person, forcing a contrived media image to perpetuate something unreal? If these questions could be adequately answered, much of the inherent controversy would subside. Maybe rock stars then wouldn't be under such stressful pressure to please, to improve, and to be everything to everybody.

In my opinion, the identity crisis that befalls John Cougar/ John Mellencamp is an internal conflict between fantasy and reality, between imagination and truth, between romanticism and naturalism. Like the working of a clock, with the ticktock of passing time, John Mellencamp is an explosive time bomb of personal contradictions, bent rules, and creative energy.

What, then, does he want to be: a romanticist or a naturalist? With all the growing up John has endured over the last two years, he is not yet prepared to answer. A naturalist would write lyrics such as the famous chorus from "Jack and Diane." No matter what happens to us, life does go on. Such a simple and direct statement captures the inherent reality of our existence. But only a romanticist would fantasize that we should fixate ourselves onto that time in our lives when we were most content. The passing of time, such a powerful reality, does not function like this.

Fundamental puritanism and his Nazarene background do influence the troubled and vulnerable John Mellencamp. A religious romantic, he cherishes life with an intensity that, at times, is difficult to understand. Yet, a lover of beauty and the past, (Mellencamp seems preoccupied with his high-school years) John professes to believe in the "Golden Gates" theme of promises made from the heart. Both of these facts indicate romantic tendencies, to be sure. But a naturalist celebrates the joys of self-indulgence, the pleasures of sexual gratification, the freedoms of no commitment, and the confrontation of authority figures. Thus far, Cougar has been more willing to allow the media to publicize his naturalistic side: the fighter, the boozer, the womanizer, the macho stud.

Fans will see a more tender, patient, vulnerable, and sensitive star. Time will provide Mellencamp with the confidence, stability, and security to do this. As he matures, moving closer to forty, this metamorphoses will be essential for survival. And nobody appreciates endurance and survival more than John Mellencamp.

John Cougar the naturalist and John Mellencamp the romanticist will, with the ticktock of time, soon establish a harmonious peace with themselves. Edgar Allan Poe and Stephen Crane would be pleased! So will John's loyal fans; we'll know the person, not an image.

CHAPTER THREE
COMING OF AGE

Enter John Mellencamp, from Seymour, Indiana, circa 1976. On October 7, 1951, exactly 102 years after the death of Edgar Allan Poe, in 1849, John Cougar Mellencamp was born to a hardworking family of Dutch extraction. Seymour is the home of approximately 17,000 people. Understanding John requires some understanding of how John Mellencamp understands Seymour. To the casual observer, Seymour is a middle-class agricultural/industrial community with green, lush farmlands sustaining a symbiotic relationship between the farmer and his land. Americans, in general, have always possessed an almost instinctual love of the land, so Seymour is nothing out of the ordinary in this respect. But all is not glittering. Chemical wastes have been dumped there for decades, prior to anybody's questioning the priority of industry over environment. The result is that Seymour, Indiana, is polluted. On this count, Seymour, once again, is not as unusual as we might want the town to be. Also, during John's teenage years, Seymour apparently held the dubious distinction of having the highest per capita murder rate in the nation.[1] Like most towns, Seymour, Indiana, is a complex entity composed of many ingredients.

John remembers: "In Seymour, kids just drive around town for something to do. If there's a gas shortage, you'd never know it. When you grew up in the fifties and sixties in that type of town, it was real important that you had these *manly* qualities. That determined your status: how fast you could run and who you could beat up."[2] Thus it appears that John ran around with a rough bunch of guys—Seymour's gang. Quite unashamedly, John admits:

> We were the ones getting kicked out of basketball games for fighting; we were the ones drinking, getting laid, getting into trouble. . . . There was dancing every weekend. We went there to fight. You *had* to fight. Your dignity depended on it. You tried to pick up girls and fight at the same time. In one of my first records I said, "If you can't find a lady, then start a fight." It was an amazing time. I had my hair real long, over my ears, but in a butch cut with a Boston Black in back, parted in front. I started putting peroxide on my hair in front when I was eleven. My folks had a fit.[3]

Young John Mellencamp was a worldly lad, albeit cooped up in Seymour. Surprisingly enough, however, rather than venture to New York City or to California, John chooses to remain in Seymour, his home and his inspiration. Seymour makes John feel comfortable and keeps him in touch with the whirlwind pace of his life nowadays. Speaking again about his decision to remain in Seymour, Mellencamp says: "I'm used to that pace of life. . . . I don't think you can take a kid from Indiana and say, 'Okay, you live in New York.' Some artists spend years trying to get away from their roots. I know when I was a kid I thought, 'I can't wait to get out of Seymour, Indiana.' I'm not trying to get away from my roots anymore, and Indiana's my home. My friends are there, and that's why I stay there."[4]

The rough-and-tough, macho drinker/fighter image notwithstanding, a mellower, more stable, more relaxed Mellencamp expresses a fear about the life-styles that many successful rock musicians live. Mellencamp blames this life-style on the overly rapid accumulation of too much money. Elegant living, in his opinion, pulls an artist away from the essence of what rock and roll is, or at least what rock and roll is supposed to be.

Mellencamp laments that all that fancy living is " . . . pretentious; it's sophisticated hogwash, and it's foreign to me. If you get too civilized and too far from the basic roots of rock and roll, you can't write and sing good rock and roll! It's one step above the gutter—not Beverly Hills! That'll destroy you!"[5] An ironic statement about his love of Seymour, to be sure. But he loves the "gutter," as he finds there the human element that makes him what he is and what he wants to be. Although Seymour is by no stretch of the imagination "the gutter," it is his home, his roots, where his family and friends are located, and where his identity, strength, and inspiration are concentrated. Alas! Seymour has been good to Mellencamp. All in all, the scales are balanced, since Mellencamp has apparently been good to Seymour.

The town itself, though, is not what attracts our musician. Towns are people: John's family is in Seymour. Just as Elvis, the rebellious son, was having a media-hyped symbolic conflict with Eisenhower, the wise father, so too did young John have conflicts with his father, Richard. After all, would you do belly flops off the ceiling if your eleven-year-old son was putting peroxide in his hair? Now in his middle thirties, John finds himself playing both roles: a son to his father and a father to his three daughters, fifteen-year-old Michelle, four-year-old Teddi Jo and infant Justice. Knowledge, however, did filter down from Richard to John. Today John says that fathering, like songwriting, is a job. "I told Michelle that just because I'm her Dad, doesn't make any big deal. Everybody in the world has got a Dad. That's when I started getting along with my Dad, when I realized he was just some guy!"[6] A masterpiece of garbled understatement, indeed! So much alienation and hurt has to transpire in our mobile society. Why can't a teenage son be a friend to his father? Why is such a relationship so elusive? Why does a boy have to become a man before he finds himself able to relate effectively to his father? The turbulent sixties didn't provide a serene, stable backdrop for this friendship to develop, but time heals the pain.

Mothers, perhaps, are able to enjoy their sons more than fathers can. Fathers want sons to be productive achievers.

Mothers are more satisfied with sensitive honesty. John's father, for example, sees John's singing career as a business. His attitude has been "Why don't you quit?"[7] After all, he must reason that John has proven his talents and made his point, so why shouldn't he stop knocking himself out and quit while he's ahead. But John's mother observes more fun in this whirlwind of success. About his mother, John says:

> And my mom, she thinks it's nice. My son is John Cougar la-de-da; she's like that. . . . She's a real snotty-nosed woman. I was teaching her about it the other day. I said, "Why do you always have your nose in the air?" And she said, "Well, you see these bags under my eyes? If you don't hold your nose this way, they sag. But if you hold it up, they don't." She's kind of a good looking woman and she likes all of this. . . . Oh, yeah. My mom's always up for an interview.[8]

Here is a woman with a keen sense of humor, a quick wit for reply, and a patient tolerance for sons.

John's father, Richard, plays a role in the running of the operation. Richard, whom John fondly describes as "one of those self-made motherfuckers,"[9] is an electrician whose diligent efforts have resulted in his becoming vice-president of Robbins Electric. Driven by intense determination and intense competitiveness, Richard—known to many as Sonny—tried to encourage competition in his sons. Young John, a short, pudgy stutterer, was not the most likely candidate for competition, especially that of a physical nature. Recalls John, "The old man would make us have footraces against each other, chin-up contests . . . you know, 'Goddamn it, John, your brother just did fourteen, you gotta do at least fourteen.' "[10] Mellencamp never lambasts anybody over something said and done in the past, with the possible exception of his first manager, Tony DeFries. (Even with Tony, however, all of what Mellencamp says is not derogatory.) With time, John the musician made his peace with Richard the electrician in the small hamlet of Seymour, a conservative, yet competitive oasis about fifty miles from Bloomington, home of Indiana University.

Technically, I guess, John Mellencamp today lives in Bloomington, but he is so close to the Seymour side of Bloomington that, for all practical purposes, he is still in the sleepy conservative bastion of the work ethic. Today John lives with his second wife, Vicki; his fifteen-year-old daughter, Michelle, from his first marriage, to Priscilla, his four-year-old daughter, Teddi Jo and daughter Justice, born during the summer of 1985. John relishes being close to his family. Rather upbeat and hip, the entire operation seems to be a family-run act. John's former wife, Priscilla, manages the office full time. His brother, Ted, is the road manager. His father, Richard, and his uncle, Joe, also play roles in the operation of the successful singing career. John tells us that success has not really had a drastic impact on his family. Reflecting a refreshingly healthy and hip attitude, John, with his feet firmly on the ground of reality, says:

> We don't use the word 'success' around here. It's more like a temporary way of life or a high point in a career. But to be really honest, I don't think my kids would know if I was successful or not. As long as Michelle's been alive—I had her when I was seventeen, and I started making records right out of college—so I've always been making records as long as she can remember. Teddi Jo's only two, so she doesn't know what's going on. She's aware, but I think she thinks everyone's dad is on the radio. I think Michelle can probably remember when her mom and I lived in a house as big as this room before we got divorced. So I think she remembers that and arguments about money. But I think the biggest thing that affects her is . . . she's really afraid that her friends like her because I'm John Cougar. It's kind of sad. But she goes to public school here because I think that's best. No big deals. I try to play it down as much as possible."[11]

Hats off to John Cougar Mellencamp for being so sensitive and loving, so open and honest. John's memory is vague, however, as Michelle was born on December 4, 1970, when John was 19, not 17. On another occasion, the singer says: "I love what I'm doing or I'd get the hell out. But at the end of the day, it is my job and that's all it is. I complain just like everybody else. I procrastinate, but when I *do* it, I enjoy it. But at the end of the day, it's a job, and if John Cougar ceased to exist tomorrow, I wouldn't go blow my head off. I'll do something else."[12] There are definite advantages to possessing two identities, particularly when the proud, insightful owner of these identities knows the difference between the two and does not hang his happiness and his psyche on the wrong one.

John Mellencamp and John Cougar are an aggressive, yet compatible duo who manage to act as a check and balance on each other, keeping the id and the ego and the superego in harmony. What John has been in the past, what he is right now, and what he would like to be in the future—three strands seem to be weaving together in harmony, tightening up to create a pretty strong fiber, one capable of handling any job and enduring any adversity.

Hindsight, as everybody knows, is an exact science. But John speaks proudly of his family: "My family were all farmers, basically of Dutch stock. My grandfather was a carpenter who never got past the third grade. He could barely speak English. My dad became a vice-president of an electrical company—one of those self-made guys. I'm the runt of the litter; everybody else had big muscles, real construction worker types."[13] Living in a town seen as being competitive; existing in a family, seeing himself as the wimp; and striving within the family to seek approval from his father—these factors must have been largely responsible for the macho-bravado style that Mellencamp projected. Survival was the name of the game in his youth, which meant that vulnerability had to be concealed. Hence the drinking, the fighting, and the prowess. But John has made his peace with his father. And fortunately, John also is finding it easier to speak proudly of himself. Witness this:

> Before I was in the business, I had zero drive. I was married with a kid, didn't have a job, didn't want a job. I was content staying home, throwing a frisbee in the morning, going out and sitting on the hood of a car in the afternoon, smoking cigarettes, doing dope, going home and eating dinner, and then listening to records at night. But I'd never be content doing that now. So that's the best thing about this career. It helps you get in contact with yourself.[14]

The last sentence flagrantly flies at the very essence of how most of us stereotype rock stars. Yet this last sentence, to me, is one of the most interesting, one of the most encouraging and one of the most enlightening insights that I have ever known John Cougar Mellencamp to utter. Here is a guy who, by his own admission, was directionless. Rock and roll gave him purpose, direction, motivation, and identity. Instead of the fame and finances destroying him, the fame and finances have put him back in touch with himself. This is tremendous! We have seen too many examples of how rock and roll and the accompanying life-style in the fast lane have virtually destroyed talented individuals. Elvis Presley and Jim Morrison are two of the most noteworthy, but there are numerous others. Of course, this marriage that John was speaking about did end in divorce, but he and Priscilla and Michelle apparently have made their peace with each other.

If rock and roll was John Mellencamp's salvation and his redemption, as I am suggesting, perhaps we are on the mountaintop, about to see a new stereotype of the rock star emerging. To me, John Cougar/John Mellencamp embodies this crossroads of transition: the former stereotype of the sexually free, booze-ridden, pleasure-seeking star is transforming into one of a more responsible, vulnerable, open, and honest individual. Teenagers aren't totally void of intelligence, regardless of how they are stereotyped. They observe the deaths of rock stars; they read about the drug-induced euphorias and the escape from reality that some stars find; they hear about the mishandled funds, so that a decade or two later, a person who should have been on easy street is filing for bankruptcy. Whatever the tear-jerking story of yesterday's stars, John Cougar-John Mellencamp is the personification of a significant change in how we stereotype our rock stars. Realize, too, that any stereotype—be it of a social, ethnic, or religious nature—is never totally accurate. Suffice here, however, to suggest that the stereotype of the rock star has always left a great deal to be desired. Suffice here to suggest that John Cougar/John Mellencamp is a symbol of that change—a responsibility inadvertently thrust upon him, but there nevertheless.

John thinks he is fortunate that the thunderbolt of success didn't strike him until he was thirtyish. Hindsight allows him to understand:

> Well, I don't know how a kid twenty-one years old could handle success. I just don't see how they could possibly be ready for it. It would have to ruin him forever, because you're pretty impressionable at that age. It happened to me, in a way. I was the complete failure, flop, joke of the record industry. But imagine a twenty-one year old kid being the biggest star of the year. I think it would ruin his entire life.[15]

Perhaps John himself was more frustrated, unstable, and insecure than most twenty-one–year–olds. Nevertheless, his observation is astute and perceptive. I've seen high school athletes having serious difficulty adjusting to the pressures of measuring up to the superstar image that the spectators want them to be. How would a run-of-the-mill twenty-one–year–old cope with this pressure? I, too, am glad that John Cougar Mellencamp's success came later in life, as the success will not destroy him. If "John Cougar" stops existing, there will still be John Mellencamp. Secondly, though, it is heartwarming to hear a rock star, a hero image to many impressionable adolescents, garner enough sophistication and class not only to realize these things, but possess the courage to admit them publicly. John Cougar Mellencamp no longer feels so inferior, so vulnerable. John Cougar Mellencamp has come of age.

This revelation undoubtedly accounts for his financial philosophy. John's organization is a family-run operation, not the corporate-type conglomeration typical of some rock stars. Indeed, John deserves applause for possessing what might be the healthiest attitude in the rock business in regard to the accumulation of sizeable sums of personal wealth. Anybody, naturally, enjoys what the money can buy. Only an idiot would deny this capitalistic fact of life. To keep his head screwed on straight, through, Mellencamp explains that this is why he or members of his family rarely refer to recent events by using the word *success*. Says the head-on-straight singer, referring to his phenomenal success, "It's more like a temporary way of life or a high point in my career."[16]

The high point is really the result of some thinking that began to brew nearly twenty years ago. Neither an athlete nor a student, young John took his peroxided hair and survivalistic attitude and initiated his personal involvement as a member of a band. He was fourteen. His memories of this are recalled with a satisfaction approaching reverence.

> The first band I was in was wild. I was only fourteen at the time and we used to play fraternities for thirty dollars a weekend. I'd do my Wayne Cochran routine and my friend, who was black, would be James Brown. We used to get the Chicago and Detroit radio stations, which meant a lot of funk and R&B. For a time, I didn't even know that white guys made records! I'd go for the guys who looked kind of ugly, like Eric Burdon, Mitch Ryder, and the Stones, You did your shopping for records at Sears Roebuck, and they weren't exactly carrying the Velvet Underground.[17]

Even hearing "Roebuck" added to "Sears" reminds me of my youth. But, alas, John was happy here. Even as a fourteen-year-old, he was learning that he could use music to enhance his position with his peers, to fatten his billfold (thirty dollars a weekend was pretty substantial pay for a snot-nosed kid in 1965), and to competitively establish his own identity.

Even at age fourteen, then, John was writing songs and forming bands, aimed at turning the world, as he experienced it, into music. At age eighteen, he left his family home in Seymour, moving to the even smaller, nearby town of Valonia. This apartment in Valonia left much to be desired, but, for really the first time in his impressionable, decisive life, John was on his own. He recollects, "It was a shack that had a refrigerator on the front porch, outside plumbing and cost ten dollars a month to rent. I worked pouring concrete and installing telephones. You might say I bombed out with this job. Once I nearly disconnected the entire city of Freeman, Indiana!"[18] Most creative souls and most intellectual minds (and I do suspect that Mellencamp is bright, even though this mentality was well concealed at school) find themselves confined with dead-end, no-future situations like John had while in Valonia. Apparently, John's soul and mind turned to rock and roll, both as an avenue of self-expression and as a ticket out of Nowheresville. By age twenty-two, he had formed his first band. The band, called Trash, was stifled since people refrained from hiring them. Says Cougar, "We dressed outrageously. We were into a Bowie type thing, but Bowie was too dressed up. Our look was more greasy."[19] Never giving up, Cougar reminisces: "I remember when I last told my friends I was gonna make a record—they told me I was full of crap. As a kid I always thought it would be nice to be a singer. But I never seriously entertained the idea because people from around here just don't do that sort of thing. They work in factories. They grow stuff on farms. They end up selling shirts."[20] Nearly an entire decade slipped through John's fingers, yet all the while, his mind was ticking and his heart was yearning. A star is being born!

New York City, circa 1975. Having been laid off by the telephone company, plus having accumulated a year of unemployment benefits, John kissed Valonia adieu and began a courageous assault of New York. The Big Apple sent chills down our hero's spine, but his dream of being a success, coupled with his determination to prove to many people that he could and would make a record, instilled him with the necessary intestinal fortitude to persevere and to prevail.

Stereotypes, the product of the mass media, again function here. All of us have an image of New York City; the city represents a cross-sampling of the best and the worse of America. New York has the theaters, the stores, the tourist attractions, and the restaurants. Unfortunately, New York also has the pimps and prostitutes, the strip joints, the street people, and the "low life." What a diverse city! Seymour's favorite son admits, "When I first went to New York to make a record, I was scared to death! We were booked into a Holiday Inn downtown, and I just bolted the door figuring, 'Hell, I don't know if I wanna do this *that* bad.' "[21] Apparently, fighting in Seymour—winning some, losing some—was not as threatening as the seamy side of life he saw in the city. Fighting people you have known all your life is never as unnerving as fighting a total stranger. Another source of fear, however, was the inner realization that when he arrived in New York City—the city of realized dreams, but also the city of dashed hopes—his accomplishments in the field of music were less than astounding at that time. John had actually written only two songs and had appeared on stage only six times. Ironically, this frightened Indiana kid, when he arrived in New York, saw some hooker beating up a john. Fear was everywhere—in the dismal external environment, in the worried internal psyche. But today John says humorously that he does not like New York; he just doesn't feel much at home there. His Dutch, farming roots are in his soul. As we know, you can take the boy out of the country, but you cannot take the country out of the boy. And Boy John doesn't even want to be taken out of the country! Again, smiling, John says, "I don't have any distaste for New York at all. I like New York. I just don't want to live there. I like going there because it's like Ma and Pa Kettle going to the big city."[22]

One of Cougar's fondest earlier memories of the home of the Yankees is his pleasant visit to a hotel suite that had been used often by Joe DiMaggio and Marilyn Monroe. Indulging a trip down Memory Lane, Cougar recalls:

> I was making a record that never came out, and I was staying at the Lexington Hotel. Marilyn Monroe and Joe DiMaggio had had a suite built for them there, and the night manager let me look at it once. Nobody stays there; it's like a memorial. The whole place was decorated real weird, almost deco-ish. And I don't know if the plastic flowers had *always* been there. . . . But the bathroom was *humongous*. You could have played football in there. And the shower was real weird. I'll bet it had five hundred nozzles coming straight up, coming this way, coming that way. There's no way your body could walk in and not get entirely wet.[23]

Here is evidence that young Cougar does have some pleasant recollections of America's most famous city. He also had a friend, the congenial night watchman. Perhaps someday the night watchman will be showing some new aspiring young musician the "sacred" suite once occupied by the renowned John Cougar Mellencamp. Probably, the plastic flowers had not *always* been there.

Soon after New York City entered into the life of young John Mellencamp, so, too, did Tony DeFries enter his life. Main Man, the company to which an innocent Indiana boy/man brought his demonstration tape, was under the auspices of this Tony DeFries. Some credit Mr. DrFries with making David Bowie the household word that he is today. DeFries listened to John's demo tape. DeFries was interested in what he *heard*, but he was even more impressed by what he *saw*. This was a momentous occasion for John, even though Tony did want him to drop the name Mellencamp, because, presumably, it was overly long, relatively non-commercial, difficult to remember, and lacking in sex appeal. John left the demo tape with DeFries, returned to Indiana, and fretted a great deal.

Varied thoughts buzzed through John's mind, as he calls these day up from his memory. Says Cougar:

> I was as excited as hell. I was gonna make a record. The guy gave us eight thousand dollars, and we were gonna make a fucking record. The whole name thing was like, well, if you want this job, motherfucker, you gotta get your hair cut. So I did it. I didn't realize it when I started, but when I thought about it—what a fucking stupid name. I didn't want to be anyone but John Mellencamp. I fought my whole life to have some kind of individuality, from grade school on up to where I am now. And that's still my greatest problem.[24]

John's vulgar language notwithstanding, his candidness here is admirable and straightforward. Yet coming to terms with the personal compromise of his individuality and of his heritage and integrity (everything suddenly began to happen so speedily) was only part of the internal conflict festering inside the young singer. Part of his confusion over DeFries hinged upon something else besides the name change. Recalling another aspect of these events, John says:

> They checked the tape out and hated it, but they thought I could sing. I went back to Bloomington and didn't hear from them. I began to get desperate. I went to Louisville, Kentucky, to a little local record company and they told me I had no talent. I was driving back from Louisville, saying I'd better get myself a job. I

got to the house and DeFries called and said:"Come to New York and let's make a deal." I told him I didn't have any money and he said he'd pay for my ticket. He paid off all my debts and bought me a house in Seymour, plus a new car. I thought, "This is the music business and I'm successful!" When I went to Los Angeles, I found out that MCA had given DeFries a million bucks for me! So he came out smelling like a rose.[25]

No doubt, DeFries did fine; on the other hand, young Mellencamp did not come out of the deal empty-handed.

In retrospect, perhaps if we put ourselves in Mellencamp's shoes and waltzed around in the playground of his active, but elusive mind, maybe it is not so unbelieveable that he harbors some hostility toward DeFries and the recording business. Relates a wiser Mellencamp: "The big distaste I have is for the record business. That's why I'm so down on big companies and promoters, and I think that's why when the record companies talk about me, they say I'm too dangerous to deal with. They say that because I'm not going to kiss ass. I'm not a hard-ass. It's just if I feel something's wrong, I won't go along with it."[26]

Along these lines, John seems to be proud of the title Little Bastard that has been hung onto him. About the moniker, he explains, "That came about because I'd go in with these big producers, and I'd have to argue with them because they'd change my songs around. I heard one of them say, 'Well, that fucking John's a little bastard.'"[27] John may have a sailor's vocabulary but he also has a sense of revelation and humor. John produced Mitch Ryder's album *Never Kick a Sleeping Dog* in 1982, and Little Bastard identifies him on the album cover. He also uses "Little Bastard" on his own record albums, so he acknowledges the fact that he does not endear himself to everybody, but prides himself on the inner satisfaction he has from being true to his Indiana background and his Mellencamp heritage.

Retelling the same story, with a slightly different emphasis, John Mellencamp relates the following:

One of the first places I took my demo tape was to Main Man

> Management, which was David Bowie's company. I met a guy named Tony DeFries who had me wait in the outer office with twenty Bowie look-alikes. With my hair the way it is now and an earring, I was the only one who looked different. DeFries agreed to record me, and he had me do a lot of strange cover tunes for an album. He also changed my name. I was John Mellencamp, and when the album came out, it was John Cougar. He said he couldn't sell John Mellencamp to the public. He told me if Cougar wasn't the name on the record, there wouldn't be a record.[28]

But John doesn't hold complete contempt for DeFries, even though DeFries forced John (as he sees it in retrospect) to compromise his principles.

As a protégé of Tony DeFries, John Mellencamp does grant him some credit:

> Oh, as weird—and condescending—as that guy was, I can't take it away from him that he was smart. He and Bowie were great for awhile, but his schemes didn't work for me. It's your motivation, and what's interesting here is that the reason you get into the industry sure isn't why you stay in it. There are two ways of looking at this. Jagger said one time, artists should make it big while they're young, because they don't understand its importance and it's no big deal. But a guy like me says, I think it's great the way I did it, 'cause you have time to get used to what's happenin' around you. It took ten years for me to have a successful record, but I've learned a lot about the business and the people and myself in that time, because it gave me time to think. For me, the long-term climb has worked out.[29]

This long struggle at least taught John to curtail his understandable ill will toward DeFries, focusing instead on the bright side. Yes, a simple man like John Cougar still manages to allow his mouth to get him into trouble, but badmouthing other specific managers, promoters, or artists is not one of those sources of trouble. This is professionalism—keeping his critical remarks general, rather than casting the first stone and compounding some past transgressions that cannot be altered anyway. This restraint is laudable.

CHAPTER FOUR

SWEET SUCCESS

After the relationship with Main Man was severed, John abbreviated DeFries's "Johnny Cougar" to "John Cougar." The first album, *Chestnut Street Incident*, was a reality therapy session, of sorts. The album did not enjoy tremendous sales, so Main Man (MCA) dropped "Johnny Cougar." He has never particularly liked the "Cougar" name, but realized the risky loss of all recognition if he released another album under a totally new surname. With all the bad breaks that had befallen John, one begins to inquire as to when a stroke of positive reinforcement would strike. Luckily, John met Billy Gaff, the manager of Rod Stewart and also the president of Riva Records. Billy Gaff possessed the integrity and courage to allow John to cut a record the way John wanted it to be cut. This album, *A Biography*, was released overseas circa 1978. One song, "I Need a Lover," became a hit in Australia. Later, a Pat Benatar version of "I Need a Lover" hit the market. John Cougar/John Mellencamp was a proven talent as a writer of contemporary songs, as a singer of modern rock, and as a force to be reckoned with.

Even in 1979, however, Mellencamp was still embarrassed when fans and interviewers would compliment him. Mellencamp would respond by stating that he was not really interested in becoming a rock star, in the normal sense of the word, and that he was "just learning to crawl as a songwriter."[1] The release of *A Biography*—while Cougar was living in London for a year or so, having moved there in 1979—allowed Cougar to discover what he wanted to do, to plan how he wanted to do it, and to figure out how to prioritize his concerns. John might seem egotistical and aggressive at times, but he learned an important lesson in both the business world and the actual world. An unknowledgeable kid from Indiana was easily swayed by the crafty DeFries. The overly anxious kid would sign anything in order to have his name on a record. Look, for example, at the number of rock stars who—before they were famous—took the advice of some manager/promoter and signed away the rights to the songs they had written. This was an easy sacrifice then, since they were told they were going to become stars. Signing away the rights seemed a small price to pay for stardom. But John Cougar, who openly admits to his mistakes and imperfections, vows never to be so duped again. His rude awakening taught him an important lesson in survival: "But the good news is that after I played that game with those guys for awhile, it brought me to my senses, real quick, and I realized that none of these people knew what they were talking about, so I might as well trust my instincts and do what I want to do and pay my own prices for my own mistakes."[2]

A 1979 album, titled *John Cougar,* was the next entrée. His first Riva album to be released in the United States, *John Cougar* contains many aggressive, yet narrative and sensitive songs. In my opinion, this album is grossly underrated, or perhaps I should say it is grossly ignored and neglected. The middle cut of side 1, called "Miami," is a haunting story about lives void of companionship and closeness, substituting superficial naturalism in their place. To me, this song emotes a tender understanding of life and a poignant perception about alienation. Next we have "The Great Midwest." The satirical treatment of the money-oriented life-style of the Midwest is described in terms of what people sacrifice for that materialism. "I Need a Lover" appears as the opener on side 2. *A Biography,* which also had his soon-to-be hit for Pat Benatar, as well as for John, was never released in the United States. Thus the decision was made to include what at that time was Cougar's greatest hit on this new 1979 album. Side 2 is my favorite side. "Welcome to Chinatown," "Sugar Marie," "Taxi Dancer," and "Pray for Me" are all worthy songs. To me, each says something to the listener, while at the same time conveying a human sympathy and empathy for the central character of the song. On side 2, Cougar deals with the sexual encounter of a young man with a Chinese prostitute, the acquisition of self-respect, the loss of a dream to be a dancer, and the admission of a personal inability to endure life's struggles alone. This is quite a panorama for one side of one album. The side runs in excess of twenty-two minutes, which is a bit of a bargain itself, and offers a panoramic view of how John Cougar himself sees life and what John Cougar himself sees as real. My only regret is that this album has been so despicably ignored; with the increasing popularity of John Cougar Mellencamp, however, I can hope that new fans will pick up this 1979 release. What a great find in a discount bargain bin! Even though the cover pictures a cigarette-smoking, unshaven, macho-greaser Cougar, the lyrics of the songs capture the essence of what really makes Mellencamp turn on to life. Maybe that's why I love the album: the *John Cougar* album is a symbolic representation of the dichotomy between John Cougar as the media sees him and John Mellencamp as he sees himself!

    This blossoming star—seeing himself as a capable musician and a creative force—simply refused to give up or give in. Ironically, during the making of the album called *Nothing Matters and What if It Did?*, John confesses that he did consider quitting. Yet listen to his reason for throwing in the towel:

> My personal life was really going well, but my record career wasn't happening. But then I decided, well, I really didn't need to work with those big timey producers . . . because it would be like you inviting me to your house and saying, "Look at this big new house I just got, John, now you decorate it!" I wouldn't invite anybody into my house to decorate it or tell me how I should live, and basically, that's what producers have always done with my songs. So, when I finally decided to produce my own records, I just said, "Look, if you're going to deal with me, you're going

to deal with me on my own terms and if you don't want to, I'll go somewhere else." And once I had that attitude, things started happening for me.[3]

Once again, Mellencamp is talking about his basic philosophy of survival: the ingredients are straightforwardness, confidence, direction, and honesty. The promising star scored two semihits on *Nothing Matters and What if It Did?*: "This Time" and "Ain't Even Done with the Night." Produced by Steve Cropper, who John says is a great guy to work with, even though the two of them think a little differently, the pseudosuccess of the *Nothing Matters* album set the stage for John Cougar's strong commercial breakthrough in 1982.

Now that John Cougar Mellencamp realistically sees himself as a pungent force in the current rock-and-roll genre of performing stars and video artists, he is mellowing. But the long haul of personal struggles and defeating setbacks taught the young man how to survive and endure on his own terms. His diligence and determination rocketed him into his status as a household name in 1982. The album was titled *American Fool*. The two rock narrative hits were "Jack and Diane" and "Hurts So Good." The culmination of their enduring climb was the winning of two Grammy Awards. This meant musical recognition from both peers and fans. This also meant financially lucrative returns. John's greatest tribute to the *American Fool* album is to acknowledge the fact that the album was a blockbusting success that brought him recognition. On the other hand, John does not feel that the overall quality of the *American Fool* album is the best he can do. Stated his way, "*American Fool* was obviously a breakthrough album for me. I decided to stop trying to be artistic like John Cale, 'cause nobody was taking me seriously anyway. So I decided to go back to my roots and write songs that you could sing along with."[4] Both "Hurts So Good" and "Jack and Diane" made the climb into the top five hits—there together, simultaneously. *American Fool*, in fact, became the best-selling album of 1982!

When John Cougar Mellencamp and his band, The Zone,

crashed into the platinum palace of successful sales and name recognition, we were lead to believe that the songs on the album were examples of John Mellencamp doing his own thing, his own way, his own style. We were also lead to believe that the title was totally, unashamedly autobiographical. With this success, however, much of the hostility and vehemence that the maverick John Cougar projected toward record company officials and press interviews began to subside. Although proud and pleased with the success of *American Fool*, the young success is still unwilling to rest upon the laurels of that one album. Quite the contrary, in fact, as he seems to demean the quality of the very album that skyrocketed him to stardom. He related:

> To be real honest, there's three good songs on that record, and the rest is just sort of filler. It was too labored over, too thought about, and it wasn't organic enough. The record company thought it would bomb, but I think the reason it took off was—not that the songs were better than my others—but people liked the sound of it, the "bam-bam-bam" drums. It was a different sound.[5]

Again Mellencamp offers a candid, honest, straightforward assessment of his feeliings about the album. Again Mellencamp resists the tendency to assume he is an established rock star just on the merits of one album.

Notice again, also, that Mellencamp has taken another step forward in refining his own personal goals and his own personal style. With *American Fool*, the record personnel pretty much let him have his freedom with the songs and their content and themes. The lyrics of the songs, then, characteristic of Mellencamp's midwestern heritage, bit into the essence of his youthful experiences and gnawed at the stark truths of reality. This made us feel both refreshed and nervous at the same time, but it also made us respond to the songs. Now, though, Mellencamp not only wants to have control over the songs and over their delivery, but he wants the record companies to cease and desist with their constant fussing over details. To John, this insistent meddling subtracts from the organic living quality of the completed album. But, contrary to what John might think, record-company personnel are not totally void of intelligence, either. They thought, *Here is a star who is now hot; here is a man who knows what he wants and how to go about it; here is a performer who, as a warm-up band for Heart, was receiving better reviews than Heart itself; here is a man who has weltered through some tediously difficult times; here is a star who will make profits for the company.* Result: *Let's let him alone to do his own thing.*

John, then, has proven his point, won a battle, and gained some strength. Realistically, though, he concedes that even now, he does not have total reign, because the business simply doesn't function that way. Even though John believes the business would probably improve itself if it did give the artists unlimited autonomy, he says:

> . . . these guys who are in power at the record companies, I think they just want to see what kind of asses they can make of themselves in a couple of years. The guy at Poly Gram now is great. He says hell, he doesn't want to see the album covers, or hear the records beforehand. We say "This is what John's doing" and he says, "Great, now here's what we're going to do with it." His rap is that records are for selling, not listening to, and for a businessman, that's a great attitude. But A and B people, who are these guys? I mean what makes them think they can call you up and tell you what to do?
>
> With *American Fool*, they just didn't like it, and they make these suggestions like "John, maybe you should put some horns on this, maybe a saxophone in the background". . . these really ridiculous suggestions. You always end up fighting those guys about something, whether it's what the single's going to be or the album cover, you know.[6]

John Mellencamp also concedes that he did not realize, for certain, beforehand, that the three songs on the *American Fool* album would become such smashing hits. Demeaning the impact of the songs—Mellencamp uses this technique as a psychological defense mechanism to help him cope with his success and to not project a pompous arrogance—John evaluates the songs as such: "I mean let's face it, 'Hurts So Good' was a cute little song, and that's about it, and 'Jack and Diane' well, there were a couple of lines that touched people, but the rest of the record really wasn't much good. There were some pretty crummy things on there. . . . "[7] John Cougar Mellencamp is being overly critical here, perhaps indulging in some self-deprecation. Doesn't almost any album have one or two lead songs, using filler of lesser quality for the remaining cuts? If John could sublimate his macho image, perhaps he wouldn't be so critical of the cuteness of "Hurts So Good" and the melodic, poignant, touching sentiments of "Jack and Diane." Yet one cannot help but admire the down-to-earth perspective that Mellencamp places upon his success.

Perhaps Mellencamp is arrogant and opinionated and confident, but he avoids being egotistical, pompous, and unreasonable. Besides, asked how he accepts and deals with his victory, he responds, "Well, it beats pouring cement. Why take it seriously? It's all pointless bullshit, anyway."[8] Perhaps our singer is not being totally honest with himself here. If this success is such "pointless bullshit," why did he endure for nearly ten years to achieve this recognition and why did he confront so many adversaries on his fight to the top? Why did he perpetuate his inner faith in himself and in his band? For "pointless bullshit"? I don't buy that, John. John Cougar Mellencamp has to be proud of his current position in the field of rock music. There is no reason why he should not be proud. John Cougar Mellencamp would do well to learn, however, to become a more graceful recipient of compliments. He seems to assume that all compliments are insincere, that they are being given for superficial reasons. As powerful a force as he is to deal with, John Cougar Mellencamp must learn to differentiate between a superficial, shallow compliment and a sincere, from-the-heart congratulatory thanks for a job well done.

Maturity plus poise plus charm are being inculcated into the diverse personality of John Mellencamp. With a recent album, *Uh-huh,* fans see him returning to his birth-given surname, but still keeping the DeFries-given stagename. According to the record jacket itself, the album was recorded in July of 1983 at a sixteen-day blowout at the Shack. The Shack is the rehearsal recording studio that John leases from his sister Janet and a friend of hers, Jeff "Poo Poo" Clark, who apparently is frequently tired. Janet was recently married, but not to Jeff. But their long friendship explains the references to Jeff and Janet Mellenclark on the sleeve of the Mitch Rider album.

This *Uh-huh* album has generated three popular videos: "Crumblin' Down," "Pink Houses," and "Authority Song." Nonchalantly, John passes judgment on the songs by flatly saying, "I think they're the best things I've ever done. But I think . . . I know, I can do better."[9] Describing the theme of "Authority Song" as "our new version of 'I Fought the Law,' " Mellencamp also pays homage to John Prine, who coauthored a novelty song included on the album. This song, "Jackie O," is one reason why Mellencamp thinks that Prine is "in the same league as Dylan as a songwriter."[10]

During this sixteen-day blowout at the Shack, Cougar and the Zone recorded twenty-five songs, ten of which were used on the album. Spontaneity, an organic quality Cougar saw as missing in *American Fool*, was their goal. "Don't fuss over everything. See how everything falls together." The formula has worked for John Cougar Mellencamp and the *Uh-huh* album! Honestly and candidly, Mellencamp says, "I'm very satisfied with *Uh-huh*. The music I'm making is the stuff I've been playing since I was a kid. It's also the kind of music I wrote when I did 'Hurts So Good.' I finished that song and everyone said I shouldn't put it out. Then it went top five. So, I figured, hell, now we're free to do a whole album of that kind of stuff."[11] Proving himself to be not only a capable thinker, but a prolific writer of songs, John remarks, "Actually, I wrote about two hundred songs for the album. I played each song on an acoustic guitar, picked up on electric guitar and added to it. One song was rehearsed at one o'clock. By three o'clock it was recorded."[12] Don't overlook the point here. John is not bragging about the speed at which he and the Zone are capable of recording songs, but he is intensely proud of the spontaneity, organic beauty, and personal empathy that appear throughout the ten songs on the album.

Continuing, John allows his pride to emerge when he talks

about "Pink Houses," one of the three videos made from the *Uh-huh* album and my favorite. Cougar talks with his simple, direct honesty, saying:

> It's saying the American Dream and all that shit is propaganda. It's not rah, rah, rah America at all, and I think it puts America in its place. It's like the Russians shooting down that plane, and we want them to apologize. I'm not condoning what Russia did, but that's bullshit! There's so many things we've done, and then we expect them to apologize when we had a spy plane beside the plane that got shot down! Let's see the deal as it really was! And the majority of the public is going to fall right in line with the way Reagan wants them to think. I don't mean to get political, but I do get wound up about these kinds of things because so many people see it as it's really *not*. They believe the propaganda. And that's sort of what "Pink Houses" is about.[13]

John's pride is evident with *Uh-huh*. First, the style of music he has been playing since he was a kid has officially been let out of the bag. Second, the freedom to write and sing and record the kind of music that he and the Zone want is a refreshing and rejuvenating achievement to earn. Third, the album itself is a personal tribute from John Cougar Mellencamp and the Zone to one of the greatest rock-and-roll bands ever, the Rolling Stones. Delicately and metaphorically stated on the record jacket is their salute to Mick Jagger and the other members of the Stones: "Special Thanks, To the Rolling Stones for never takin' the livin' room off the records when we were kids." What a complimentary and sincere way of applauding the Rolling Stones for sticking close to their roots, for doing their own thing, and for remembering what the recording business was all about.

Only one disappointment surfaces with the *Uh-huh* album. But, alas, this disappointment is an external one, not an internal one. For the video of "Authority Song," John apparently hoped that Burgess Meredith would show up and was disappointed when he failed to do so. Luckily, the one disappointment on the album is cosmetic, not substantive.

It had been a tumultuous, exciting climb to the mountaintop, so to speak. On the mountaintop, however, John Cougar Mellencamp sees clearly, thinks clearly, and plans clearly.

What looms on the horizon for John Cougar Mellencamp? John still struggles with his inner frustrations. Ironically, success does breed problems and create responsibilities: both for the star and his loyal fans. Risking criticism again, John confesses:

> I was having problems after *American Fool* came out because all of a sudden I turned into the guy I hated—the guy who's on the radio all the time and the guy dealing more with business sometimes than music. It was hard for me to deal with, and I think writing "Crumblin' Down" helped me. Because when the walls came crumblin' down—when all the bigtime deals fall through—I'm still going to be "the same old trouble you've been having for years." So why the fuck are people treating me differently? What's the big deal? People seem to be more affected by what they think I am than I am about the whole thing myself.[14]

Hooray for the honesty here. But also note the frustration. Mellencamp is justifiably proud of his crowning achievements to date, yet insecurely battling the changes the successes generate. Look, John, at any high school football team. When they are suffering through a miserable, degrading, losing season, the bleachers on a windy, snowy Friday evening are largely deserted. Oh, sure, the band is there, the parents of the team members are there, and a few of the most dedicated fans are there. But, for the most part, the empty seats outnumber the occupied ones. The ticket-takers are not so busy, and the athletic director is worrying about making the program a viable, self-supporting sport. On the other hand, when that same high school football team is winning all of its games, the team members are racking up impressive individual and collective records and are being seen by scouts for college and maybe even professional teams, and the sweet smell of victory is felt by everybody in town, the empty seats fill up. The band plays to a capacity crowd, the parents see more of their friends and neighbors, the ticket-takers are kept busy, and the athletic director is relieved of his financial woes. The same scenario occurs with any sport, even in college or on a professional level.

So, aren't you being a bit naive, John, to be so critical of the people who treat you differently? You are a recognized star now, instead of a struggling musician. We always treat winners differently than we treat those who have not yet proven their worth. Like it nor not, more is expected of somebody who has proven he can pull his own weight, somebody who has shown that he is capable of competing with the best, somebody who has indicated his abilities and has been duly recognized by the public. You are a singer and you say you want to sing, that you resent all the business that consumes so much time. This cry is heard by people, no matter what job they have. How much time does a building contractor actually devote to building? How much time does a lawyer actually spend in a courtroom, displaying his legal expertise? How much time does a cement-layer actually devote to laying cement? A schoolteacher only spends about one-third of his or her total time at school actually engaged in the art of teaching. Any job involves shuffling papers, tending to business, and dealing with interferences. Besides, I can ask a thousand weekend bandsmen if they would be willing to change places with you, and you know what their answer would be. Accept the changes and revel in the glory.

Besides, you, yourself, are changing, too. By your own admission, you are trying now to create songs that have even more to say, that have some particular relevance to a certain point in time, say 1985. Nobody stays the same. Don't insult us by expecting us to believe that you are not different. Time changes us all. The goal is to become better with the passing of time. You are doing this. Don't give up and give in. But, also, don't wallow in an infantile mud hole of self-pity. You are a rock star. You are a businessman. Challenge the stereotype of rock stars being totally void of all intelligence and virtually lacking all class. Be true to your yourself: allow the kid inside to grow up, without giving into whatever you really feel is wrong.

No doubt, well-meaning fans and good-intentioned folks are all asking John for this and for that. Such is one of the prices one pays for success in a field such as rock. But consider the alternatives, too. The expectations and obligations that ride in the saddle with success are sweeter to travel with than the obscurity and neglect that sit in the valleys of forgotten dreams. Ahead, then, lies the necessity to come to peaceful terms with all of the aspects of the business.

What else looms on the horizon for John Cougar Mellencamp? Like an exceptional student who has great difficulty deciding his college major, because he is well-versed in so many areas, John Couagr studies his options:

> I've got a lot of things I want to do. I'm starting to dabble in a lot of things, like rock video, and I've had numerous offers to produce records, since *American Fool* and Mitch's. And sometimes I entertain the idea of finding an act and just producing like Peter Asher did with Linda Ronstadt. I'd like to find some new kid who's hungry and help him because—let's face it—you've really got to be hungry to stick in this business. But, hell, who knows? Maybe I'll end up like Charlie Watts—nearing fifty and still rocking strong. I can't see myself doing that right now, but who knows? I'd like to be able to make records as long as I want and quit when I want—not when I *have* to quit because nobody buys them anymore. Or keep making them 'cause they're breaking my arms to make them. I guess I'd most like to be like an old soldier and just fade away. Because there's a lot more to life than playing in a band.[15]

Autonomy—to make his own decisions, rather than to have them thrust upon him—carries considerable weight for our paragon of contradictions from Seymour, Indiana.

One thing seems obvious, however: John Cougar Mellencamp, if he desires to do so, will be here in one capacity or another. Most obviously, he can continue as a likeable, yet particularly untamed rock star. Second, he can work behind the scenes, producing albums for others. He produced Mitch Ryder's *Never Kick a Sleeping Dog.* Even though the album has not shown amazing sales, it has accomplished what it set out to do. The alleged purpose of the album was to reintroduce Mitch Ryder and the Detroit Wheels in a reunion type of record album to accompany a promotional tour. Third, John can continue his artistic endeavors by producing rock videos for other artists. He has already illustrated his laudable abilities in this area, so he certainly would not be held in disrepute as a producer of the new art form of rock videos. Fourth, John could discover a new talent and concentrate his efforts on the development, production, and promotion of that one act. John claims to enjoy working with "hungry" newcomers to the business. And, fifth, John could follow in the steps of other rock stars and start a movie career. To this end, Larry McMurtry has read and edited a screenplay John wrote during the summer of 1984. Dealing seriously with downward mobility and the rippling effects on guys John's age, John's screenplay needed McMurtry's help. Now John laughs when he confesses that he would understand if Warner Brothers wanted somebody else to star.

Howard Koch, Jr., a film producer, allegedly sought John as a star for *The Idolmaker*. True to form, John turned the part down because he'd be required to shave and cut his hair. Quips John, "I've had some other offers, too, but I'm not really interested. Maybe if the right people approached me, who knows? I wasn't considered for *Eddie and the Cruisers*, though they say the guy's supposed to look like me. Poor ugly dude!"[16] About the movie offers, on a similar note, John says, "I heard there's a movie out where the guy's supposed to look like me. Ugly fucker, eh? [He laughs.] Well, I hope he gets laid more than I do. I've had a few movie offers, but I'm really not interested. Maybe if the right people approached me, but the stuff I've been offered is stupid."[17]

No doubt about John's flamboyant nature, his informal tone, and his sexy aggressiveness being film material. Let's hope, however, that he continues to scrutinize the movie offers that flow his way. When he wants to venture into a movie, let's hope that John uses his brain, nurtures his strengths, and accepts a movie that will be a decent finished product. If the movie he was in were a humongous flop, such a disaster would not, of course, terminate his career as a rock performer. But should the movie he was in be a box-office smash—both artistically and financially—credence would be added to his ornery confidence; credibility would be added to another niche for the Little Bastard who has already snatched two platinum rings. John's aggressive, boozy voice, his poignant, sensitive perceptions, and his memorable, definitive stature and appearance will serve him well in movies. His debut as an actor will be eagerly awaited.

A soothing comfort reigns when fans realize that the talents of John Cougar Mellencamp are diverse enough and strong enough to guarantee him a place in the business: as performer, producer, talent scout, promotor, and/or movie actor. John thinks that his opinion of the record-company personnel has not really mellowed over the years. Whether he is accurate or not in this assessment is open to speculation. But John does provide an optimistic comparison between them and himself. Note the sense of permanence that transcends this statement: "Like I've always said: Most of these guys wouldn't know a good rock song if it bit 'em on the dick. They're pompous, they're self-serving. But now, yeah, I've come to see they're basically insecure about the position they're holding at that particular moment. They just don't know how to act, so they come across real arrogant and condescending."[18] Pause a moment here and reflect. I feel like a priest hearing a confession from a young man who is insecure, unsure, and scared. But read on, MacDuff, and harken to the optimistic appraisal that John gives of himself. This is one of the rare occasions when John offers himself a pat on the back. "Let's face it—most guys in this business last two years, and then WHAM—so long! I've been at my label a long time, and I've seen 'em come, and I've seen 'em go."[19] And, according to John, this rapid fall will not happen to him "if I stay close to my roots. I've lived in this same house for the last eight or nine years, out in the country near a lake. It's a college town. . . . I actually stay home a lot—I'm a very reclusive person. I function best that way, and I get my strength from this. If people like the music that comes out of this, well then, that's fine with me."[20] John enjoys having hailed from Seymour, battling recording executives, writing hit songs, proving himself, and living in Bloomington. Let's hope he continues to do so. Keeping tuned in on the Indiana "rebel with a cause" is entertaining as well as enlightening.

CHAPTER FIVE

THE GUY I HATE

Who, exactly, does John Cougar Mellencamp hate? As a kid, John suffered from an intense inferiority complex. Some say he still does. As a struggling musician, John perpetuated a macho-man image of booze, knuckles, and women. As a successful recording star, John acquired a reputation for being intolerant of recording-company personnel and various professional interviewers. Now, as an acclaimed rock star, John copes with all the problems that fame generates. Now, in interviews, John laments the reality of success. He patronizes others in a condescending manner; he ignores some people with an aloof conceit; he manages a multimillion-dollar enterprise, frequently losing sight of rock and roll in the process; he works at protecting his privacy, without alienating his fans. As with all endeavors, success brings additional demands. John Cougar/John Mellencamp has not yet clearly decided how he will field these requests. But he recognizes that he cannot always handle them the way he would prefer. So, whom does he hate? The inferior, competitive adolescent? His misguided macho image? The recent star? The promotional image?

Let's try to see this from the perspective of John Cougar Mellencamp himself. Vulnerability, for example, is a dominate concern. Riding the success wave of *American Fool*, John sometimes wondered, "Where do I go from here?" Imagine: here was a singer and his band who had released three albums in the United States. *Chestnut Street Incident,* the first album, spearheaded a grand promotional push at the 1976 Oktoberfest in Seymour. On Saturday, October 2, Johnny Cougar and the Tiger Force Band played a nine o'clock concert at the local National Guard Armory at Freeman Field. Five-dollar tickets purchased a single admission to the concert, plus a copy of the album. After this local hoopla, the album accomplished little. Then, three years later, an album called *John Cougar* appeared on the scene. Proving satisfactory, the album remained on the *Billboard* charts for seven months. Not bad at all! Its best ranking was position thirty-two. But "I Need a Lover," a single, climbed to number nineteen. Next, fans enjoyed another palatable course, *Nothing Matters and What if It Did?,* a 1980 release. Two cuts, "This Time" and "Ain't Even Done with the Night," entered the Top Forty charts, and the album hung in on the *Billboard* charts for over eight months. Even at this point, with two successful albums under his belt, Cougar told a local reporter, Jim Plump, "You would think that would give you more confidence. But right now, I'm worried about the next record. It's got to be good."[1]

In retrospect, John's remark proved to be a superb example of understatement. The next album, *American Fool,* made John a star. Musically, the album was a personal triumph; financially, it was a lucrative gold mine. But all that glitters is not golden. The 1983 release, *Uh-huh,* was a straightforward, no-hype album that was successful, yet not as phenomenal as *American Fool.* Place yourself in John's position. Relate to the pressures regarding the next release, reportably due on the market by the summer of 1985. If this new release sells even fewer copies than *Uh-huh,* what would that mean? Artistically, a fine product does not necessarily cash in with the public. Some will say, however, that Cougar's career was on the skids if this album was not a commercial success. On the other hand, an album that equaled or surpassed the impact of *American Fool* would enhance and cement John's newfound prestige in the world of rock and roll.

Previous to *American Fool,* Cougar thought his career would continue as it had been going: his albums were mildly, yet unspectacularly, successful; his enthusiastic voice was regularly heard on the radio; his sales were profitable. Assessing his career, John says:

> I was used to having my records get into the Top Twenty for a few weeks, sell maybe 400,000 copies and that would be it. I just figured that was as good as I was going to do, and that was fine with me. Suddenly, things all changed. I never realized there was such a difference between selling 400,000 albums and selling 800,000 like this one. The difference is that once you make the Top Ten, the airplay and the recognition you get increase tenfold—and people start treating you different.[2]

As an English teacher, I wish John would use "I" instead of "you" when referring to himself. As an average man-on-the-street, I find myself lacking sympathy, but understanding the problem. Coming to grips with one's own success always requires adjustments. Is it possible, though, that John could have been so innocently naive about that for which he had been inwardly yearning? Quite honestly, Mellencamp confesses, "In some ways, I guess I'm afraid of this newfound success. I know the pitfalls and the evils that go with it. It's like, oh shit, do I really want to deal with this? I was quite content before this happened."[3] Nobody, of course, knows exactly what the future holds. The American dream, though, causes us to expect progress onward and upward. Even John's personal goals must include his accepting these new challenges, proving his adaptability, and persevering in the business. Perhaps a rock star never totally escapes from these fears of vulnerability. John possesses the talent and the stamina to endure; he merely needs time to internalize the meaning of stardom and redirect his efforts to these obligations.

Will this level of reorganization and renewed commitment be possible for a boy/man whom the media portrays as a self-indulgent, outspoken, substance-abusing punk? John's self-indulgence comes to light with his pleasure-seeking sexual habits. Possibly, John's sexual behavior was a form of personal rebellion against Nazarene morality, as well as an avenue for asserting a competitive manliness. Mellencamp has been married twice, first in 1970 and again in 1981. Both brides were pregnant at the time of the wedding, approximately two months along in 1970, nearly full-term in 1981. In this day and age, this hardly seems shocking. But John makes frequent, off-the-cuff remarks about "getting laid." One former employer relates a humorous story about John. This remarkable, congenial lady loves John like a son, but also recognizes his foibles. John, it seems, was always disappearing from the job, so she had to seek him out. On one occasion, he was found in the basement of the house they were painting—indulging in his sexual lust. With tongue in cheek, the boss, showing great tolerance and admirable patience, announced, "I don't mind you screwin', John, but I don't like paying for it." This woman has a way with words, plus an empathy for young men who sometimes are caught off-guard. Even John must have been speechless in this embarrassing situation.

On other occasions, though, Mr. Mellencamp has shown himself to be quite outspoken. The incident on "CBS News Nightwatch" when John became outraged at a persistent line of questioning is now a well-known, yet still unfortunate, event. Explains John:

> It was the woman not accepting my answers. She asked me the same question five different times, I answered it five different ways, and it was like hey, what the fuck else do I have to say to you? Don't get me wrong—you know from talking to me today that I'm definitely for women having equal rights, but this woman had equal rights and being a bitch mixed up. She kept saying that I had responsibility to my audience, and I kept saying, "No. I do what I do, and if kids see me as a role model, then it's wrong, because I make a lot of mistakes." I answered it that way once, she asked again, so I answered it a different way. I answered it five times, and finally—I thought it was on tape, it wasn't live—I said, "Fuck it. I don't need to get on national TV and argue with you. Forget it!" And the total pimp job was that they ran it the day [publicist] Howard Bloom was in negotiations with them on what we could do to reconcile the situation.[4]

Dressed casually in baggy sweatshirt and kneeless jeans, Cougar was relaxed and comfortable until Felicia Jeter, the interviewer, objected to a sexually lustful video ("Hurts So Good") that portrays women in leotards and chains. Suggestive? Of course. Enjoying Cougar's amorous attention? Yes. They were paid to do so, or at least anxious to volunteer to be included as part of the video. Perhaps Cougar was right to object to Jeter's continuous questioning along the lines of her objections, but on the other hand, the questions should not have rattled John as much as they did. When I see John being interviewed on camera, even speaking to a relatively local audience, he seems uneasy and awkward. Talking to interviewers is not his bag, yet the obligation goes with the glory of stardom. In any event, Jeter drilled John about the fact that he was now establishment, that he had responsibility. Then a thirty-one–year–old married man with two daughters, John retorted, "I don't go to PTA meetings. I don't go to the Nazarene church. I don't vote. I don't do any of that stuff."[5] Outspoken John seemed satisfied, but a shocked Jeter pushed on. Spouting vulgarities, Cougar exited halfway through the taping.

Who is to blame? Felicia Jeter, for asking the questions? John Cougar, for losing his cool? Does either party have to be at fault? Today, under the same circumstances, John would have become uncomfortable, but would not have become so unnerved and would not have made such a spectacle of himself. Since the segment was not live, why not stop cameras, resolve the problem, agree to continue, and prevent the fiasco? John frequently refers to himself as an idiot, a runt, a simple guy, and by other such less-than-complimentary adjectives. His distaste for authority and his need for understanding frustrate "the kid inside." He does not have to give in, but John Cougar Mellencamp does have to grow up.

Cataclysmic outbursts like these will diminish in frequency. The *Indianapolis Star*, after hearing about their rock-and-roll bad boy throwing an infantile temper tantrum, contacted the assistant producer of *"Nightwatch,"* Michael Stone. Over the phone, Stone commented:

> We've had hundreds of calls, very emotional ones. I heard from some people who had tears of joy over the way she handled it, and also from professional rock 'n' roll people who pointed out that rock stars are a little bit fragile and shouldn't be made uncomfortable. There are others who say it's not our job to make people comfortable. Then there was another person who suggested that "Mr. Cougar might have been a little wired."[6]

Speaking to Jill Warren, the reporter who wrote the article for the *Indianapolis Star*, Michael Stone adhered to a strictly factual, nonjudgmental account of the unfortunate incident. Stone even refrained from offering any commentary—positive or negative—on whether or not Cougar was on drugs. Felicia Jeter, the interviewer, also offered some insights into the flare-up:

> Poor guy. . . . The tact I was taking had to do with adult responsibility, the fact that he is now a grown-up. He *is* one of the people that his music has been rebelling against. He's establishment now. He talked about it for awhile, but then it got to be more than he wanted to talk about.
>
> I think maybe those questions had been going through his own mind and they were problematic for him. It was probably a combination of a lot of things: His own immaturity perhaps.
>
> He called for his PR guy to make me stop like he was a little spoiled baby. But he was great up to that point, a real sweetie.
>
> A lot of entertainers are concerned with an image of being just plain Joe, and that's impossible. Being bigger than life is a problem for some people. But that's what he is. People who don't acknowledge that are living in some kind of a dream world.
>
> I think one of the reasons this interview bothered him was that it was not fitting with his PR image. I wasn't going along with the picture of himself he likes to portray in public. I made him uncomfortable.
>
> It was not what I'd consider a heavy pressure interview. If I had really put the guns out, he'd probably have run out screaming. I was just being persistent.

> When we have entertainers on our show, it's not about *who* you are as much as how you fit into the fabric of America and why people think you're important. We ask a different kind of question.[7]

Felicia Jeter, in my opinion, is on target when she suggests that John Cougar Mellencamp suffers from an identity problem. In another interview, John's mother, Mrs. Richard L. (Marilyn) Mellencamp, spoke about an operation John had. Born with a growth on his back, John, as an infant, underwent a serious operation that could have resulted in paralysis or even death. Once he had returned safely to his parents at home, Marilyn remembers, "I waited on him hand and foot. He is spoiled to this day. He was a difficult, demanding child. He wanted everything a minute before you did it. He wanted to be the center of attention."[8] No doubt, Felicia Jeter will accept this appraisal!

Untangling such a spontaneous mishap is akin to separating a bear from his honey. Like all of us, though, John learns from his misfortunes. Dismayed, John recollects the incident and admits that he should have known better than to allow himself to be swayed into doing something he did not want to do. John's publicist thought that such an interview would "open doors," but John was tired, anxious to have the interview concluded. While he waited to go onstage, John read the teleprompter, which was billing him as "John Cougar, the cat of rock and roll." Bewildered, John asked Felicia Jeter if she would be kind enough to keep the interview light and easy. Everything progressed satisfactorily until a decision was made to extend the interview. Then, according to John, she "unloaded on me" with questions about the sexual connotations of the "Hurts So Good" video.

To some the "Hurts So Good" video demeans women. These critics claim that the video from John's hit song perpetuates a subordinate sex-partner image of sadomasochism. The adoring females are skimpily clad, with chains rattling. The macho guys ride motorcycles. Frankly, if I were a cycler, I might object to the stereotyped image of the easy rider. Nevertheless, the video became controversial, much to the chagrin of those involved. For a while, at least, the sensitive programmers at MTV banned the video. But if one considers the fun-oriented, albeit sexual, lyrics, the visual backup of the video itself comes over as more of a campy put-on than a feminine put-down. Yet I have difficulty believing that John was so naive that he did not anticipate some objections to the content of the video. The song itself was hatched before the video came along; the song was also a hit. The song, in my opinion, deserved a less sensationalized video: the attention should be directed to the song, not the video. This preventable fiasco focused the media's attention on the video, a situation that seems to detract from the essence of what rock and roll was meant to be. The lyrics, which are not objectionable, are laudable rock. Occasionally, even now, MTV does run the "Hurts So Good" video. For the viewers who see the video as a humorous spoof—as I believe it was intended to be—the men *and* women are then laughing at their antics and at themselves, *not* demeaning each other.

Pan in on London, Ontario, not too long before this *"CBS News Nightwatch"* nightmare. According to John, somebody talked him into doing an August 30 concert that he did not want to do: the booking agent was the fast-talker on this foul-up. Ticket sales for a concert by the Beach Boys and Del Shannon were faltering, so John reluctantly agreed to be added to the billing. On tour with Heart at the time, John, at first, wisely refused. Then, since August 30 was his day off and since the promotors agreed to supply equipment, pressure was exerted and the refusal to be added to the billing was reversed. As per Murphy's Law, the situation deteriorated from bad to worse. The rented equipment was inadequate, and the promoters reduced the time alloted to John from fifty-five minutes to a thirty-five–minute set. Since ticket sales more than tripled in volume after John's name was added to the program—from two or three thousand sold to ten thousand sold—John concluded that the fans were going to blame him for the ten-dollar price for a thirty-five-minute show. All of these variables festered inside until they exploded onstage. John's version of the mishap goes like this:

> So we went on stage, and the minute [guitarist] Mike hit a chord on his amp, it broke. That's the kind of junk they rented. I spent most of the time fighting microphone cable because it was all fucked up. The PA system was inadequate, and we're thinking this is what these people think we do on stage. The longer I was up there, the more angry I got. So finally, I just said "Fuck it!" I went through this long spiel about how promoters are fucked up, and then we put all the equipment he'd rented that had fallen apart—it was junk—into the audience. So there was some kid there that night who left with a bass drum, or a cymbal or whatever. And it was inaccruate reporting, because we didn't *heave* it out in the audience. We handed it to security guards who handed it out to the audience.[9]

The memorable lessons of life crystalize in mysterious ways; for John Cougar, this lesson was a costly one: he returned to London for a free concert (his atonement to the fans), he paid for the drums and the PA (his expiation to the promoters), and he was never paid for the original concert, such as it was. Nonpretentiously, John tenaciously admits that he learned that he would have to be careful about what he verbalizes onstage. Anybody who believes that character and nobility are nurtured only through personal struggles certainly must be placing their money on Cougar to "win." Alas! The kid is growing up.

Shedding more light on the London concert—still another unfortunate affliction to the identity problem of John Cougar Mellencamp—John upholds his behavior by explaining in more detail (or at least with different emphasis) his position. Once onstage, John learned that the PA system was inadequate, as the audience could deaden the sound so that the band would not be heard. Even the microphone was too cheap to do a decent job. Frustrated and angry, John then asked those in attendance if they had come to see his band. More than half of the audience showed their enthusiasm, which irritated John even more, as he thought he was going to be identified with and blamed for the rip-off. Fans of his had shelled out money to see him; then his set had been reduced to a mere thirty minutes. So John told the fans that he felt they were being ripped off. However, John denies having thrown a drum into the audience, and he denies any injuries taking place. John says he handed the drum kit into the audience. John's ultimate defense is that he would have been sued if he had injured anybody.

Perhaps John as a pontificator, pompous and dogmatic and all, does not set well with some people. And, no doubt, John's image would be less distorted if these flare-ups could be grappled with in a more stable manner. But, in fairness to him, these preventable mishaps damage John and his image more than they hurt anybody else. How can anybody, for example, refute John's logic when he asks, "If somebody got hurt, don't you think they'd have sued me right away? Rich rock star, let's get some of his money."[10] This seems especially plausible in this day and age, when so many lawyers are willing to accept cases on a "no win—no payment" basis. Even a slight injury would have given birth to a lawsuit: the attorney would receive publicity, the client would receive financial compensation, and the media would receive still another opportunity to publicize the stormy side of rock concerts and rock stars.

But even this narrative has a humorous conclusion. Every incident possesses an element of laughter. Every situation has a comic relief, to help release the tension and defuse the bomb. After his temper tantrum, John walked backstage, where the Beach Boys and the promoter were standing. Still fuming in anger, John coaxed them into saying something to him. One of the guys broke the ice by saying, "Nice show, Jerry Lee." John laughed. Ultimately, however, John says he reimbursed the promoter for the drums and the PA system, but was never paid a cent for the concert. To make good on his promise, John also claimed he was going back in April for a free concert. Even amidst this chaos, John remains proud of the fact that he is still popular as a musician and as a performer. Projecting his adolescent defiance of authority, John is pleased that he can play by his own rules and still succeed.

Mr. Mellencamp's outspokenness, coupled with his inherent Bohemian outlook, was a source of turmoil long before Felicia Jeter and concert promoters entered his life. Just how outspoken was John while in high school? Being caught with a pack of cigarettes at football practice resulted in John's being kicked off the high school football team during his freshman year. As he hailed from a family of "physical, construction types," as John refers to them, and saw himself as a runt, this ejection from the team must have been a blow to his ego. And, as we have observed, even in his thirties, John doesn't internalize attacks on his ego particularly calmly. For numerous adolescent males, football is an approved, glorified, institutionalized method of exerting physical force and proving manly qualities. While visiting Seymour, I spoke to John's freshman football coach, who remembers John and revels at his current success. Whenever his former coach is asked what kind of football player John was, the man told me that he answers, "John wouldn't hit anybody unless they were smaller, and nobody was smaller. He was all boy and got into scrapes. He played halfback position."[11] Perhaps John wasn't playing by the rules of the school and the athletic department, but was he successful with this venture? Football was apparently somewhat important to him as a source of prestige, yet that ambition fell victim to cigarettes. (His trademark Marlboros?) At age thirty-four, John must recall events like this when he sings about fighting authority, arrogantly taking pride in the fact that he always loses.

Another teacher in Seymour remembers John in a more academic environment. Playing the class clown, John did what was necessary to earn a "C." Beyond that, John showed little motivation. This teacher attributed John's attitude to a lack of interest, not to a lack of ability. As a teacher myself, I know this type of student is more common than we would like to admit. John's teacher recalls him as an energetic youth who was "smart and quick-witted." But, as with many teenagers, John apparently found it more fun to go downtown, sit on cars, and watch girls. Fondly remembering a likeable John Mellencamp, the former teacher, smiling, says:

> If you could accept John as he was, a happy-go-lucky kid, and

laugh with him—you did okay. John always sort of lived on the edge. He knew when to stop and not go over the edge and get into trouble. He knew what he was doing and knew just when to stop. I always had the impression that outside the classroom, he was hell on wheels. Nothing would surprise me about his after hour activities. I was, though, impressed with his persistence and the fact that he stayed with his roots. John liked attention, he liked to get laughs, but he was not dumb. In many ways, he was a pretty smart boy. Quite poetic, he has a way with a phrase.[12]

According to *People Magazine,* John's affinity for confronting authority did include run-ins with school officials and legal authorities. My visit to Seymour produced no allusions to the altercations, which tells me that, whatever they were, they were relatively minor and best forgotten. John, projecting his characteristic hedonistic indifference, told one reporter:

> I caught grief for having a big mouth all my life. I got in trouble in school, in trouble with record companies—I always say what I shouldn't say. I'm too stupid to shut up. . . . I had more fun than ten kids in New York do. I hate to sound like a pompous ass, but I think we definitely got more girls than those kids in New York. We'd also get drunk four days a week. . . . When you get older and things start to change, it is weird. It is hard to be happy. I have never had a full good day since I was twenty-one.[13]

Why does John persist with such statements? This remark was made by a boy/man who was about to turn thirty-one. Why is John still so vulnerable, so intimidated, so scared? Ironically, these qualities might be partly responsible for his populist appeal. Don't we all see a little of ourselves in the manchild who shoots off his mouth, even when he would serve his own best interests by remaining silent? But even as a teenager in Seymour or now in his thirties, why was/is he competing sexually with his New York counterpart? Why was/is his self-esteem defined in terms of scoring with more females than the adolescent boys in the Big Apple did? Even if this inane competition were rational, how would John know if he were "getting" more girls and drinking more booze than some teenager in the faraway city? Why is John obsessed with refusing to grow up?

What does John Mellencamp now fashion as the "real" him?

Admitting that he has a problem with image, John seems unable to determine for himself what image he feels comfortable with. This fondness for projecting a devilish brat image is contrasted with mellower moments, when John portrays himself as a relaxed, honest businessman who enjoys his roots in Seymour and his ties to his family. Regardless of which image is being nurtured, however, interferences always muddy the waters. Had John been primed for the line of questioning from Felicia Jeter, on *CBS News Nightwatch*, the infantile outburst of obscenities might have been averted. Felicia was interviewing the establishment businessman while John was being the rebellious punk. What image does John like? What image does John hate?

When will this identity crisis be resolved? When, in fact, did this identity crisis begin? Today, John frequently refers to his youthful days in Seymour. Rock fans have heard a multitude of recollections centering upon fighting, drinking, and whoring. The runt of a physically strong family, John was encouraged, and perhaps even pushed, to excel in athletics. But these expectations never developed into anything out of the ordinary. During his early years in high school, John worked for his uncle, who is in the concrete business. He hoped John would train to become an exceptional athlete, so steps were taken to toughen and strengthen John's muscles and stamina. Consequently, people would see John behind a wheelbarrow filled with cement—running! To the observer, such a sight must have been humorous, but did John sincerely want to become a seasoned football hero? Did John see this as humorous? Or was John trying to live up to the expectations of people he loved? During lunch, the cement crew would rest under shade trees. John, however, was supposed to toughen himself by remaining in the sun. When hauling forty-foot forms on a chain, John was expected to ride the forms—to build leg muscles, to improve general posture and stability, and to increase endurance. John must not have objected to this informal training program, yet he wasn't pursuing his own dream, either.

One wonders exactly how tough John Mellencamp was during his junior high and high school days. His own remarks would have us believe that he eagerly sought fights. At least one person in Seymour told me that some of the guys who knew John during those years take exception to his media-hyped macho image. According to this source, John was so physically short and small that many of the guys could throw him; they did not tremble in fear over John Mellencamp whipping their ass. According to other sources, however, John was one strong hombre. Where does the reality stop and the fantasy begin? Recently, John has talked about how uncomfortable he felt being in a boxing ring to shoot the popular video for his smash hit "Authority Song." Now, one would think that an avid fighter like John would at least not be uncomfortably intimidated within a boxing ring. John told the video jockey from MTV that the director kept yelling at him to look angry, but John claimed he was not angry. To this, the VJ chided John a bit, saying, "What do you mean? I understand that you can really get down." While speaking, the VJ clenched his fist and sportingly boxed at John. Embarrassed, John sheepishly attempted to downplay the reference to his physical prowess.

A former English teacher remembers that neither academics nor athletics was John's forte. On the other hand, this teacher sees John as a class clown seeking attention-getting laughs, not serious trouble. Speaking fondly about John, the teacher reminisced: "John presents the image of being rebellious and a nonconformist like James Dean, but in school he really wasn't like that. He was pretty normal. He had a good sense of humor, and he liked to have a good time."[14] Other teachers in Seymour related similar recollections. John did not frequent the public library, seeking knowledge. However, he was a likable, fun-loving, personable adolescent.

These qualities allow these professionals to speak admirably about John now, over fourteen years after his 1970 graduation from high school. John takes pride in his statements about how boring he thought Seymour was and about how he refused to play by school rules. Such refusals culminated in his dismissal from the freshman football team, but the teachers find it difficult to remember John as the roughshod troublemaker that he claims to have been. Maybe the teachers are being forgiving, neglecting to bring to mind any sordid details, relishing, instead, John's fantastic success and attesting only to his more refined and acceptable antics.

So, once again, in still another context, the identity crisis perpetuates itself into a greater absurdity. Like a resolute potentate, John says:

> Everybody in town always looked up to me for encouragement. If I could get away with it—long hair or something—then everybody else could get away with it. We played at being hoods. We were the ones getting kicked out of the basketball games for fighting. We were the ones getting laid. We were the ones with access to booze. I'd get real drunk and get in some kind of fight every week.
>
> A lot of parents used to tell their kids not to hang out with me, . . .that I was a bad kid. "He'll get you arrested." I wasn't bad really. They just didn't understand me.[15]

Note how John admits to the fighting, the whoring, and the boozing—three manly, macho qualities, perhaps, but not the self-indulgent behavior that teenagers are encouraged to discover and to experience. Talking from the other side of his mouth, though, John asserts that he wasn't a bad kid, just a misunderstood one. Numerous references along this line of defensive thinking surface in John's popular lyrics. Even at age fourteen, when he formed his first band, John specialized in a less mainstream type of music. In fact, John claims that he was never a strong fan of Elvis Presley because Elvis was too pretty. John always admired what he called the ugly guys: Eric Burdon, the Rolling Stones, and Mitch Ryder. Precisely what image does John desire, though? How does John see himself? Even when John addressed the issue in past interviews, one questions whether he was speaking from the sincerity of his heart or to the pressure of a media promoter. Claiming to have hitched his career image to a group of Seymour's rebellious fringe, Cougar adapts his loser-identity deportment and proudly asserts that he was never a potential member of Demolay. He liked to fight, as often as five times a week. He and his buddies liked to go to the Elks Club and roll their parents' cars into each other. The fun of shifting the transmissions into neutral, then shoving the cars down the hill still brings pleasant memories. John remembers an older guy with greasy hair. This guy had hit a teacher several times and could be observed drinking on the corner at noon. John claims that this individual was his role model. Fondly remembering his youth, John says the most interesting people he has ever met are the guys he grew up with in Seymour. Seymour expected individuals to compete and to make a mark for themselves, according to John. With John and his friends, their worth was a result of their badness: talking fast, drinking hard, and scoring big with the girls. Peer pressure to create a stigma convinced John that he should frost his hair, cut one side shorter than the other, and wear an earring. The boss of the paint crew, the lady who found John in the basement enjoying another sexual encounter, is the one who pierced his ear. For the midsixties in Indiana, John's behavior and his appearance must have attracted considerable attention and even greater chagrin. Excessiveness was the name of the game, and John knew the rules all too well.

An older, wiser John Mellencamp admits, today, that when the macho front is stripped away, a vulnerable individual is exposed. Like James Dean, an apparent hero, John seems to be a rebel without a cause.Why is John so vulnerable, so scared, so insecure, so unstable? When will the "real" John Mellencamp hit the scene? When will the necessary courage and the needed confidence blend in harmony to squelch these Bohemian images to a rock beat? Even if these images are accurate, they are subject to change. As a thirty-four–year–old rock star, John needs to resolve his public-relations problems. Already, the blue jeans and T-shirt are giving way to more conventional attire. When I saw John for the first time at the Fox Theater in Detroit, on March 29, 1984, he began the concert performance dressed in a gray corduroy suit. He did not wear a tie, but at least this image was more compatible with his age and his responsibility. My students were astounded to learn that I was attending a rock concert, particularly one given by the foul-mouthed, outspoken Cougar. But the worse word John uttered was *hell*. The image is being groomed anew, into a cleaner, more conservative mold. My hunch is that this change of pace is a conscientious effort, an intentional ploy. Nurturing the "corporate image" is a necessity!

Seeing himself as a simple, honest man, Mellencamp becomes increasingly bothered by the negativism in the press—especially when the reporting is distorted and/or inaccurate. True, John perhaps does little, if anything, to enhance his standing with the media. But, being a man of action, John suspects that actions will prove mightier than promises. John is shedding his naiveté about his coveted stardom. Before he became a household word in 1982, John would generally conclude a concert performance by yelling to the fans, "If you see me on the street, say hello. If you're ever in Bloomington, stop in." Obviously, this act of showmanship has been discontinued. Fans can understand this. John's initiation rite into the realities and the problems of rock stardom is not yet a completed one, but the rite of passage has carried him beyond the threshold of self-knowledge and self-awareness.

At long last, perhaps for the first time in his life, Johnny Mellencamp is learning how to like himself! Here is a young man who did everything wrong, according to our traditional pattern of successfully achieving the American dream.

John didn't take studying too seriously. His grades, although unimpressive, were adequate enough for him to enroll in Vincennes Junior College, in Vincennes, Indiana, where he graduated with a degree in broadcasting. This education was financed through loans from the government and a rehabilitation scholarship. Surprisingly enough, John had a stuttering problem. Maybe this is why he liked to sing: any stutterer I have ever known is able to sing without stuttering. In any event, John did not directly associate his personal success with extraordinary academic achievement. His scholastic performance resulted in a diploma, but his transcript of credits is, apparently, unimpressive. He performed at whatever level was necessary for him to endure and to survive. Broadcasting was never viewed as his ticket to success; broadcasting was more of a second-choice alternative if everything else fell apart.

John also never seriously sought athletics as an avenue to achieve recognition, earn scholarships, and meet girls. As he was physically diminutive, fame on a football field was unlikely to materialize, even though he played some football. As I mentioned before, his ambitions were thwarted when he was bounced from the freshman team for possessing cigarettes. One former buddy told me that John, while in junior high, kept to himself, not really having a whole lot of friends. John did, nevertheless, run the 100-meter and 200-meter on the track-and-field team. Some recognition would result, but once again, John's perserverence and determination were not adequately taxed by the athletic arena. When he wanted girls, he didn't need an athletic letter. Instead, he would "scoop the loop" along Chestnut and Main.

Let's not lose our perspective here. The vast majority of teenagers are neither athletic heroes nor scholastic Einsteins. This is nothing unusual or out of the ordinary. On the other hand, John seemed to be living a "seize the moment" philosophy of hedonistic self-indulgence. Obviously, this would be a source of irritation to his parents. A few weeks prior to his graduation from high school, John ran away to Kentucky and married Priscilla Esterline. Their daughter, Michelle Susanne, arrived nearly seven months later, on December 4, 1970. Michelle was born in Seymour, at the Jackson County Schneck Memorial Hospital. Although they were divorced in 1981, Cil (as Priscilla is called) works for John. Michelle lives with John and his second wife. Priscilla is older than John: how much older is open to speculation. One source says three years older, another says five years, while still another sets the age differential at eight or nine years. Let's use the lowest number, three. In May 1970, when Priscilla was pregnant with Michelle and married John, he was eighteen (he would turn nineteen on October 7) and Priscilla was, let's say, twenty-one. What rational parent would be ecstatic and delighted over this marriage? Even Marilyn, John's mother, remarked that the last thing John needed was another mother.

Then and now, John had a way of marching to his own drummer. He worked for the phone company, bringing home $135.00 per week, until he was fired for using offensive language to customers. He worked for his uncle also. (Now, as a success, John laughingly told Dick Clark that he couldn't understand why fans shelled out dollars to see him in concert. "They could have watched me pour cement for nothing a couple years ago," says John, again mocking himself).[16] Periodically, however, John was unemployed, so the burden of carrying the financial load fell upon Priscilla. She worked at a local downtown shoe store. Today, John regretfully admits that Michelle must have overheard arguments about money (or the lack thereof). John claims that he enjoyed tossing a Frisbee with his brother, doing dope, and working on music. Who would lay odds on the domestic future and the financial stability of this family? Here is a man (boy) with a family who enjoys playing with his Frisbee.

Reluctantly, John's father, Richard, eventually lent his son some money so John could travel to New York with some demonstration tapes. (Until recently, Richard was an electrician, carving his way into a vice-presidency. Financial and legal problems created difficulties with the electrical firm, so Richard, too, now works for John.) One can understand how Richard would be pretty bummed out with his son when John was younger. Richard would undoubtedly prefer a son who was going to become a doctor or a lawyer or something at least more "masculine" and respectable. No doubt, a successful rock star hauls in the dollars, but what were John's chances for success?

This is an American Horatio Alger story, however; Richard's initial loan/investment has paid handsome returns. Life throws many curveballs. Richard assumed that John would never succeed as a rock star, so he never offered any encouragement. He and Marilyn rarely frequented local bars, such as the Chatterbox, when John and his band were working for fifty bucks or so a night, on Friday and Saturday only. John Jay Mellencamp was the oldest son of Richard L. Mellencamp. (Joe, an older brother of John's, is from Marilyn's first marriage.) Many a father has endured disappointment when a son does not live up to the vicarious expectations he holds for the boy. Many a father harbors dreams about his son accomplishing even more with his life than the father was able to do with his. Richard was, no doubt, a typical father. But the postwar baby boomers witnessed a different, permissive society and an unstable, complex economy. These variables, plus John's uncanny determination and persevering self-indulgence, drove a wedge between father and son. Enter shades of James Dean, with a lack of communication and understanding between dad and lad. Time, bless her, heals wounds. Like Priscilla, Richard now works for John, so the relationship must be harmonious, albeit awkward, occasionally.

In one interview, young Mellencamp also confessed that he never understood his mother either. Is it any wonder that this boy/man has an identity crisis and an image problem? He doesn't always understand himself either! Progress is being made, however; besides, over the long haul, one might be a better person when this self-revelation occurs a decade or so late. Who knows?

Unlike Cil and Richard, John's mother, Marilyn, does not work for John. She works for the post office, driving a rural mail route. Marilyn has described John as a quick kid who jumped around, a strange boy, and a spoiled child. Candidly, Marilyn admits; "I never encouraged John, because I went through all of that as a swinger myself, and it takes you away from things you shouldn't miss in life. I already had one son, Joe, in rock and roll [Joe Mellencamp, ten years older than John, recorded a couple of albums with a band called Pure Jam], so I was ready. I didn't know John was going to be a star."[17]

Marilyn justifiably frets over the adverse conditions and negative stereotypes that typify show-business personalities. Alcoholism, drug addiction, paranoia, loss of family ties, being away from home, pressure, identity problems, conspicuous consumption, escapist fantasies—these would worry most any mother. (Actually, Joe is closer to being three years older than John). Two years ago, when just beginning his quest to cope with his newfound success, John remarked:

> Sometimes lately, I've been tempted to start drinking again, which is something I haven't thought about in ten years, because it's real hard to relax and this crazy stuff keeps happening. Like a while back, my wife and I went out to a Ponderosa Steak House for dinner and about fifty-nine people asked me for my autograph. It was sickening. None of my friends want to go out to eat with me now. And every day, about ten or twenty people drive through my driveway. I've had to put in a security system and everything.
>
> The wierdest thing, though, happened a couple of weeks ago. I was standing on the street at Seymour, Indiana, talking to my brother, when all of a sudden three high school kids ride by on motorcycles and this one kid yells, "I'd like to stomp John Cougar's ass." All of a sudden it's like I'm sixteen again. I found myself saying, "Fuck you, you little SOB!" Then I thought, "What am I doing? Here I am, thirty years old and wanting to fight some kid." That was a really hard thing for me to realize about myself, that some kid can pull my trigger like that.[18]

Introspection is never easy, but it is always worthwhile. Of course, this particular high school biker was probably issuing a challenge, based upon John's media-hyped image. The bottom line is that John Mellencamp is growing up. A certain degree of jealousy lingers, however. Perhaps this is why Seymour has not supported John as enthusiastically as one might think the city would. Localities, mocking the 1976 release of the *Chestnut Street Incident* album, would sing, "I'll beat my meat on Chestnut Street, do-da, do-da." But, as any musician will attest, "making it" is the name of the game.

The sacrifices that "making it" requires place an unbelieveable strain upon a marriage, leading some musicians to the conclusion that music and marriage don't mix. Consequently, some folks blame music—with John's ambition and dedication—for the destruction of John and Priscilla's marriage. Others, without placing blame, merely feel that it is a shame that John is no longer married to Cil. Until John made a success of himself, Priscilla's parents (her father died from a heart attack a couple of years ago) and Cil herself supported John. Thus their reasoning is that John perhaps would never have become successful if it were not for Cil and her parents. And, according to one local man, the guys who want to kick John's ass today are the struggling musicians who are jealous over John's success, since they were unable or unwilling to make all of the necessary sacrifices, to pay the price, *and* the college graduates who played by all the rules that John ignored, but who are not relishing the financial returns that John is receiving.

John married for the second time in June of 1981, weeks before his second daughter, Teddi Jo, was born on July 1. John's second marriage is with a woman seven years younger than he. Vicki is lucky in that she did not have to endure the frustrations of poverty. However, unlike Cil, Vicki does have to cope with the lack of privacy that John's stardom has generated. John relates an incident that is becoming increasingly common: "I like to shop with my wife, but if we go to a mall, within ten minutes we look back and there are fifteen kids following us and whispering. Vicki got so mad one time she stopped and walked back to 'em and said, 'Look, we're not deaf. If you want to come up and say hi, come up and say hi, but don't follow us around the mall.' It gets to be a drag."[19] At first, an outsider's reaction might be something short of sincere sympathy. After all, John is a wealthy man, largely as a result of loyal fans such as these. These curious onlookers follow John and Vicki throughout the mall because they are enthralled over being close to their famous hero. This momentary proximity provides a temporary elation for the admiring fans, but it deprives Vicki and John of a restful afternoon of shopping. The loss of privacy is frustrating, forcing them to become reclusive, staying home more often than they would prefer. John Cougar is not the first rocker to experience this unfortunate twist of fame, however.

John enjoys living in Bloomington, however, because he loves his roots and he loves his home. As a celebrity, though, he finds it increasingly difficult to conceal himself from his fans. Regardless, John will live in Indiana as long as possible. Residing near a lake, he regrets that he will have to move because his wife cannot breathe with so many people around all the time. Well-meaning fans think *Let's go visit John*. Not wanting to criticize his fans nor dampen their enthusiasm, John does wish that they would realize that all these people stopping by the house are a nuisance. John realizes that he would be nothing without his fans. But even these loyal devotees drive him crazy at times. For example, John will be barbecuing something on the grill when, suddenly, a dozen or so strangers appear. Gone are the days when John would end a concert by saying to his fans, "If you are ever in Bloomington, stop in for a visit." Fame, plus a more domestic life-style, make this type of closeness impractical. Thus John resigns himself to the reality of eventually moving again, staying secluded until fans track him down.

Originally, John and Vicki, along with Michelle and Teddi Jo, resided on a few acres of wooded property just a stone's throw from the popular tourist area of Lake Monroe. Believing that affluence would corrupt, as well as remove him from the essence of real rock and roll, John said that he could not see himself living in a house better that the $65,000 home he had. With three televisions, a car, and several motorcycles, John was content, even though he confessed that his house was a "dump," according to the standards of Los Angeles. But John loves his "dump." However, frequent interruptions have persuaded John to move from this first home to a $180,000 residence about six miles away. The former house now serves as an office. Indeed, John loves the Lake Monroe area of Bloomington. The fans still seek him out, but the security system offers the Mellencamps additional privacy. And we have to give John credit for understanding and appreciating his fans, even though he becomes frustrated over their antics. Taking the uninvited visitors in stride, John tells how they like to test the security cameras. "I'll just be getting to sleep at about 3:00 am, and I'll hear a bunch of people outside screaming, 'Hey, John, let's party.' It doesn't bother me because I just turn over. But somebody has to tell them to get out of here, and it turned out to be Vicki's job."[20] Lucky Vicki! But, if John were really serious about becoming a recluse, about concealing his whereabouts from his fans, he could button up on national television and in rock magazines and stop spouting off about the fact that he lives in Bloomington. Yes, incidents like those mentioned are inconvenient and bothersome. On the other hand, the shortsighted fans mean no harm, as they react to a media-hyped image of a partying playboy, stopping to visit their heartland hero. Subconsciously, John must realize this; the fans made him what he is!

The proverbial bottom line is that the fans are fun. And, according to Mellencamp, enjoyment is what the rock-and-roll rat race is all about. People who earn large sums of money frequently say that the money itself is not a prime motivating factor. Claiming to receive his kicks from the challenge, John resolutely mocks lavish living as he grandiloquently explains that extravagant living can ruin a rock and roll star. Pretentious money is alien to him, as he prefers the earthy image of earlier rock and roll. A sophisticated, affluent life deadens the spirit, so John tosses this type of life aside. Chasing the American dream, earning vast sums of money, and bathing in status and prestige mean nothing to John Mellencamp. Enjoyment keeps John going, not a desire to be rich. If he wanted to be rich, John has said he would be selling cocaine or something like that, not performing rock and roll. Yet he understands that his denial of living the elegant life will culminate in some criticism. Fans might observe him driving a Ferrari and residing in a bigger, more costly home. He might be accused of "selling out" his convictions to the temptations of money. Worse yet, John will think that the criticism is justified, which will make him sad. When one earns more money, after all, one is bound to spend more money. Conspicuous consumption, to be sure, is an American hobby.

Indeed, nobody questions John's raw and earthy demeanor. Nor does anybody ever claim that John lacks spirit. To me, John is a contemporary personification of the American dream becoming a reality, although he might resent the analogy. And let's be realistic: human nature thrives on status and prestige. Some would even suggest that he has already sold out.

Yet John Cougar Mellencamp is being amazingly honest when he says that enjoyment and challenge are his battle cries.

Fans cannot believe he would ever be a cocaine dealer, and even though wealth may not have been his driving force, he must be a rich man by now, and he must admit that affluence certainly beats poverty!

Has young Mr. Mellencamp sold out already? In other interviews, John has spoken about money. Even when he was married to Cil, when money was scarce, John claims to have spent *everything*. Recalling the royalties he received from Pat Benatar's recording of his song "I Need a Lover," John humorously rambled about his need for more money, claiming to need more motorcycles. The three he already owned—a Harley Sportster, a Suzuki PE 250, and a Yamaha Scrambler—were not enough. Five thousand dollars would purchase a Harley Double Bubble, with 1200 cc. Speaking soon after the release of *American Fool*, but prior to knowing about the platinum gold mine that the album would become, Mellencamp confessed that he needed to save some money, that he needed to cease his habit of earning five dollars and spending ten.

Describing himself as an "American fool," John accepted his Grammy Awards attired in faded blue jeans without knees. Most of the others attending the gala television event were dressed to the hilt, putting on the ritz. True to form, with a candidness that becomes a bizarre combination of arrogant dogmatism and populist charm, Mellencamp's acceptance speech consisted of a mere seven words: "What can I say? I'm an idiot." Again this simple directness amuses some, infuriates others. Patience must reign, however. Our blue-jeaned Peter Pan is tottering; growing pains are offering insights; our thirty-four–year–old hero is crossing the threshhold of maturity. Lackadaisical remarks, like the one above, are now being overshadowed by a wealthier, mellower, more mature individual who measures his personal success by a different barometer.

Perfectly good days elude the young songwriter, so he is left with fantastic moments, not great days. Connecting all the fabulous moments together for a once-in-a-lifetime kind of day would be great. Ruefully, Mellencamp surprisingly admits that his records mean nothing; happiness is his quest. Reading about the success of *American Fool* in *Billboard* is fine, but now that money is no longer a problem to him, his priorities have changed. Having enough money to last the rest of his life has allowed young Mr. Mellencamp to see beyond the Harley Davidsons and the music world. Once again, he reaffirms his commitment to stay in Indiana, avoiding both Los Angeles and New York, in his concentrated effort to avoid being another casualty of the fast-paced whirlwind-world of rock and roll stars.

Statements such as this reflect a John Mellencamp who is largely unknown to many fans. Instead of the obnoxious, rebellious brat, this comment shows a surprisingly aware and remarkably sensitive man. Stringing all of our "fabulous moments" together, for a great day, is an intriguing concept, an interesting perspective on the daily routine of living. Then a rock musician confesses that records and music are not the dominant forces in his life. Even John was becoming so honest and serious that he scared himself. Thus the comic-relief reference to the Harley. And typically campy Mellencamp is the love-of-living concept; a rock-and-roll casualty is something he will never be. John has remarked that even if "John Cougar" would die tomorrow, he would still be John Mellencamp. Amen for such a healthy attitude to the sudden stardom he has experienced.

For some reason, I am convinced that John Cougar Mellencamp is serious when he says that the accumulation of unlimited wealth is not his goal. How many men, at age thirty-four, however, are in a position to never ever work again, should they not want to? The American dream lives—in Bloomington! Have you ever written to the Cougar Fan Club, using the addresses printed on the record sleeves? If you wrote, wouldn't you expect a response? Not a personal letter from John, of course, but wouldn't a fan expect a form letter, thanking him for appreciating John's music and offering him various promotional items to purchase? Such a response is merely corporate merchandising. Rock stars do not always enjoy the metaphor of the corporation, but it is a valid comparison. To date, my writing to the Cougar Fan Club generates no response. This practice will change at Cougar and Company, as ignoring the fans is rude. Worse than that, though, ignoring them is lousy business. Fans anticipate a corporate response; so provide one. A corporate response beats being ignored. This fracture in the corporate empire is being sealed, so fans will probably begin to receive a response. Yet enhancing his financial coffers doesn't seem to be John's goal. Rest assured that the coffers will benefit, but a star has to appreciate his fans. This, apparently, is the motivation for rearranging the fan club.

Other evidence, besides this example, indicate that money is not John's lifeblood. First, John refused an offer to become spokesperson for Honda. Because he has always preferred a Harley Davidson, he chose not to participate in the advertisement. Back in the days when he was smoking Camels, John says that Camel Cigarettes offered hundreds of thousands of dollars for him to star in their advertisemant campaign. But the slogan "What the real man smokes" did not appeal to John, so he rejected the offer. Success breeds lucrative offers, apparently. Something went amiss with the plans for John to compose the theme song for *Tootsie*. He also passed on a role in *Chain Gang* and a role in *Private School*, where he would have portrayed a nineteen-year-old virgin who was also a voyeur. Cougar had his head on straight when he turned these bombs down. Besides, how could Mellencamp be convincing as a virgin, or as a nineteen-year-old, for that matter?

Astute and shrewd enough to realize that a stinking movie role could spell ruination, John is talking with screenwriter Zalman King about a nonmusical movie. This role will prove to be a sizable challenge, the type Mellencamp thrives on. Since the fighter felt uncomfortable in a boxing ring, *acting* a part for the "Authority Song" video, a special challenge will emerge. A nonmusical will test his capabilities as an actor, instead of causing him to follow the pattern of so many rock stars who delve into movies. Frequently, the quality of the movies endures *only* when the musician is singing. In other words, the rocker flops as an actor. John Cougar Mellencamp possesses sufficient moxie to become a reputable actor.

Details about the movie are vague, but local rumors do circulate in his hometown. First, one rumor suggested that the title of the movie would be *The Kid in the Cage* or something to that effect. A second rumor had it that shooting would begin in September or October 1984 in Seymour. Still another rumor heard said the theme would lean toward an autobiographical concept. Possibly, John would be playing a big shot in high school. (His runty size does have some advantages, as do his boyish looks.) His parents are affluent and his closest friends feel "important" just to be seen running around with this high school hero. Yet, alas, this protagonist learns about the dismal reality of life. Even though his life had not been the best, nor the most productive, it hasn't been all that much of a misdeal either. He has held a pretty strong hand and is learning to play the hand effectively. A fourth rumor is that Sean Penn will star in the movie. One other rumor claims that guitarist Larry Crane has written the theme song and that John himself will at least assist with writing the screenplay. Should these rumors prove to be reliable at all, the movie should fare pretty well.

My hunch is that John Mellencamp will be a box-office draw and a convincing actor, partly because he is so accustomed to not taking himself too seriously. I hope the movie will prove successful, both artistically and financially, and will differ from previous movies that featured rock stars. So many of these genre flicks are predicated upon the same story line. All that changes from film to film is the rocker who is inserted to be the star. I hope experience has instructed John not to divert his energies. John's first love is music; the movie, surprisingly, will be a non-musical. John must not allow his commitment to the movie to divert his creative energies from his next album. An acclaimed movie will pay tribute to his career, but his next record album needs to surpass *Uh-huh* in popularity. John proved his talent with the success of *American Fool* in 1982, yet an established rock star has to prove his staying power by constantly releasing successful albums.

During the spring of 1982, when *American Fool* was released, John was adjusting to having turned thirty years old the previous October. Little did he know that the album would generate a need for considerably more adjusting. Mellencamp knows how to capture and enthrall an audience, but suggests that he does not overly concern himself worrying about long-term fame. Quite humbly, John has said that the guys in The Zone, including himself, are a small band from Indiana; they are not great musicians, to be sure, but fortunate enough to have a hit record. It seems that 1982 had been a phenomenally great year. Other than that, John negates the idea that he is a star. Even in a decade, enjoying similar success with each album, John doubts that he would even then be a real star.

In the driver's seat, John has stated that he has never wanted to be a "rock star." On the other hand, success breeds confidence and still more success. In the rock-and-roll genre, growing older can be a threatening reality, but an increasingly impressive number of rock stars are in their forties. Even so, teenagers maintain their loyalty, as they listen to some of the rockers that their parents were listening to twenty years ago. John Cougar Mellencamp and the members of The Zone need to decide upon some long-range goals. At least one member of The Zone, Larry Crane, works on solo albums, so he must have some alternative options, should Cougar and Company fold.

Larry Crane has been with John for nearly fifteen years, on all the albums except *Chestnut Street Incident*. Smiling proudly, Larry's mother remembered the early years, when Larry still lived at home, would move away, then would return. "Larry's mattress traveled down the hallway many times," laughed Mrs. Crane. She remembers when John used to sell albums from his private collection in order to make money for demonstration tapes. He lived in a shack, ate beans, sold albums, and paid the price for success. According to Mrs. Crane:

> Nobody really had faith in John. He is a plainspoken, outspoken person. I've had him in my home many times. Strangers dislike him, but Larry is loyal to John. Larry is laid-back and easy-going. He and John are complete opposites. John is good for Larry and Larry is good for John. . . . John is a very sensitive person. He does not take criticism well. . . . He becomes upset about bad reviews. "Hand to Hold on To" describes John a whole lot.[21]

Indeed, Larry and John are a workable match. They must see eye-to-eye on most matters.

Regardless of the harmonious relationship between John and Larry, members of the back-up band (not always named The Zone) have changed frequently. After the promotional flop of *Chestnut Street Incident*, some members departed out of frustration. With lukewarm success, some members developed a nonproductive, callous attitude. Explaining, John again attacks those musicians who are in the business for fame and riches. According to John, one should be in the rock and roll business because he or she likes the music. Liking the money, cocaine, and easy sexual contact is okay, but those cannot be the overpowering reasons for staying in the business. Earlier, a couple of members of the band started to act like famous rock stars. This lackadaisical attitude angered John. Wearing sunglasses and fancy haircuts in and around the studio, getting into too much cocaine and booze, staying up all night—these behavioral problems disturbed John, especially when the guys would walk into the studio at eleven o'clock, then moan about not being in the mood to record. John always retorted with the admonition that they had better snap into the mood pretty fast, as the studio was costing $175.00 an hour. Becoming the authority figure that he generally defies bothers Mr. Mellencamp also. But sooner or later, one has to learn the difference between work and play. Fun is okay, but not when it interferes with work.

John Cougar Mellencamp is playing the heavy, being the authority figure, forcing a business decision, and firing band members! What an establishment role to play! Indeed, the kid grew up. Perhaps this is a role he hates, but he'll grow accustomed to this adult figure. Does John realize how much he sounds like parents and teachers with this attitude? All evidence indicates that John and his father are not particularly close, even though a mutual respect exists and allows Richard to work for John today. Acknowledging this relationship, John confesses that his feelings for his father are enmeshed within his combative attitude. John admits that he owes his dad a great deal, even though, as a teenager, he hated his "old man." Richard, according to John's perspective, was opposed to everything John liked—rock music and long hair in particular. John always believed he could whip anybody because he could withstand punches from Richard, who was considerably bigger than he. Being five-foot-seven and weighing 135 pounds since he was thirteen years old, John saw himself as a tough guy, even though he really wasn't. Ironically, John was the biggest kid in his class when he was thirteen; but by age fifteen, the other guys had grown bigger, while John stayed the same. Thus those who had been beaten up by John two years earlier found themselves, in high school, in a position to even the score. According to John, most of them took advantage of the opportunity. Even as a teenager, though, John Mellencamp seemed preoccupied with an obsessive desire to prove himself to those who resided in Seymour.

John had to prove himself to the Mellencamps also. When John was seventeen, his father, Richard, was vice-president of a sizable electrical company. Somewhat impresed over the fact that this company helped build the Superdome in New Orleans, John still finds it difficult to relate to this kind of existence. Cougar has sometimes joked about the concept of success in the United States. He says we are supposed to keep our noses to the grindstone, hoping that by age fifty we have a halfway decent job. At age fifty, Richard had achieved this; two or three years later, Richard was working for his son. Father and son now understand each other better than ever, but whenever John speaks about his father, images of James Dean float through my mind. Any son has feelings of affection for his father, but John's teenage years were from 1964 to 1970—troublesome years, to be sure. The first marriage did nothing to improve the conflict of the generation gap, but the marriage might have kept John out of the army.

The turmoil whetted his insatiable desire to succeed. Music, it seems, really is a meaningful element of John's life, not a mere ticket to fame and fortune. The music is serious to John, but this lesson in priorities reveals why the business aspect of pumping the publicity machine and pleasing the company promoters is not his favorite bag. Buckling under to the dictates of the industry itself—sacrificing the soul of his music—must be refused. John's best lyrics are those that uncover emotions, that deal with people. He is not the social commentator of rock music. Maybe he will move in that direction, but even when he does (and I assume he will), he will probably do so with a feeling of people in mind. John has stated that he would never write a song about some political upheaval in some country like South Africa because he would probably be incapable of truly understanding the situation. But as he develops a greater social conscience, my guess is that fans will hear some lyrics about *people* thrown into these social upheavals. The lyrics will shy away from fornication and other such topics that have launched John's enviable career.

Becoming acclimated to being in his thirties has also enhanced John's wishes to be a praiseworthy father to both Michelle and Teddi Jo. John is a highly affectionate father to four-year-old Teddi Jo, nicknamed Butch. Teddi Jo is lucky enough, however, to never have known a life-style typified by occupational, domestic, and financial problems. She will only know a successful, tender, loving father who devotes whatever time he can to her. Michelle, on the other hand, is witnessing the transformation of her father. In 1970, when Michelle was born, John was too much of a kid to be a strong father. He had no job, nor did he have a calm relationship with his own father. Today, Michelle lives with John, Vicki, and Teddi Jo, and Justice. This provides John the opportunity to be a father to Michelle, to atone for some previous errors, to devote more than lip service to his patriarchal role, and to enjoy benefits of being a father to a teenage daughter. As a father of two daugthers, I find this American dream to be both heartwarming and (in John's case) symbolic of a refurbished image.

Vicki, John's second wife and the mother of Teddi Jo and Justice, is the daughter of a Hollywood stunt man. She probably comprehends the tribulations that afflict those in the public eye of the lucrative world of show business. Since she is seven years younger than he is, Vicki allows John to feel younger. With such support, coping with his thirties will become easier. Vicki can be there as John redreams his dreams and redirects his goals. Adulthood plus fathering plus stardom all shower one with responsibilities and obligations. John certainly has been symbolically cleansed with all these showers!

Maybe these three cleansing elements will result in fewer mishaps. The daredevil in John might take a backseat. Riding a cycle alleged to have been a wedding gift from his parents, John experienced a life-threatening accident. After rehearsal one night, he was joyriding, showing off his motorcycle, traveling seventy miles an hour. When he was about to hit fourth gear, he sighted a "fuckin' dog" in the middle of the road and hit the "son of a bitch." John slid nearly 400 feet on the motorcycle, fell off, and skidded on the concrete. Although his knee was in pretty tough shape, John thinks he was pretty lucky, because he was not wearing his helmet. Later, after everybody knew that John would fully recover, he was told that one of the guys in the band, who was following directly behind in a van, had said that he would probably lose his bonus because John was certainly going to be killed in the mishap.

Somebody up there was smiling upon John's countenance. In "Danger List," John refers to Jesus Christ. The Big Man, as John calls Him, must still care! The dog John hit, an Airedale, lost its life. John lost his kneecap; sliding across the cement burned a hole thorugh his skin, straight through to the bone. Excruciatingly painful as this was, it is better to have the knee absorb the beating than to have his head skidding across the cement. John was still on crutches when the recording of *American Fool* was started and when he fired two band members for becoming too much like stars. Trouble sure does fall upon John in bundles.

All of John's experiences and feelings provide the material for popular lyrics, however. As John's maturation process continues, not only will we hear fewer pseudoshocking obscenities uttering from his mouth, but his appearance will also adopt a flair that is more typical of a man into his thirties. To some extent, this transition has already begun. With Crepe Soul, an early band, John's dress was far out, but remember that the covers of

Chestnut Street Incident and *A Biography* reflect a blue-eyed and sensual John Cougar.

Maybe, too, John will grow to accept himself as a writer. He once mocked those who saw him as a writer, because he believes it is pretentious for him to call himself a writer. He scoffed at a critic who once referred to him as the Tennessee Williams of rock and roll, sneeringly suggesting that such an analogy was superfluously absurd. Fearing that fans will take him too seriously, John says that he uses his lyrics to communicate a simple idea that people tend to overlook. According to Mellencamp, his songs deal with the insignificant aspects of life and reality. Tennessee Williams and Richard Brautigan are serious writers, whereas John sees himself as one who has a great time making a living.

The living, as we all realize, has been pretty decent, particularly since *Americam Fool*. John's younger brother, Ted, like Richard and Priscilla, works for John. Ted is the tour manager. Ted told one interviewer that John was excited about purchasing a $2,800 Jet Ski, since being "able to afford fun" was a new pleasure. Ted also says that of all the traveling John has done, he likes Rome the best. Now, with John's musical ambitions and his financial goals pretty much established, Ted assesses his boss as being pretty much like everybody else, in that his wife and three daughters are of primary importance now. Fame has forced John to remain at home a great deal, yet a reclusive mentality has not become a problem. John has his family and friends, plus his materialistic possessions, to keep him company. A satellite dish provides all the necessary media entertainment, and the rolling hills around Lake Monroe supply the cycle trails. A close friend of John's told me that John is trading his 1963 Corvette for a tennis court. So, yes, life does go on!

Success has had a positive impact upon John, contrary to the negative impact that living in the fast lane has had upon so many of our rock-and-roll stars. Perhaps John is correct when he says he is pleased that his breakthrough came when it did, when he was thrity-one. A somber John Mellencamp wonders if it would have destroyed him had it come a decade earlier.

Only time will reveal whether the boy/man who shared top male rock vocalist honors with Rick Springfield at the tenth annual American Music Awards will be successful at assimilating a symbiotic harmony with his affluence and his middle-class heritage *and* with his multimillion-dollar enterprise and his antiestablishment pose. Talk about contradictions; one nearly bursts out in tears of laughter when John asks how such a simple guy can get into so much trouble. Ain't that America, John?

To me, the future of John Cougar Mellencamp and Company is a healthy and stable one. John has learned a great deal about many aspects of the business: promotion, production, location, sound, lighting, editing, and merchandising. Oversights are being corrected. John has also learned to admit he has erred. Speaking to Christopher Connelly, a writer for *Rolling Stone,* John mentioned the burst of obscenities on the episode of "CBS News Nightwatch." "I ain't gonna hang on nobody's cross," remarked John.[22] A clever metaphor and not exactly an apology, yet, time has erased much of the furor. About the London, Ontario, tirade against the promoters, John confessed to the fans, when he returned for two makeup concerts that he had "fucked up," and that he had returned to Ontario to balance the scales of justice. During the performance of "I Need A Lover," his first smash hit, John was even able to joke with the audience of fans. Laughing, with tongue in cheek, John kidded the audience by asking if it was the proper time for him to toss the drums into the audience.

John's publicist, the Howard Bloom Organization in New York, certainly realizes that John knows how to run the devil bowlegged. For a while, in 1983, the Bloom Agency announced that Mr. Cougar would refuse all interview requests. Going incognito, with a low profile, was a shrewd maneuver, as somebody who longs to become an established star needs to avoid further squabbles and outbursts. As Ted Mellencamp observed, they are involved in big business, so the days of fun and games have ended. John, in fact, hopes to be able to experience all aspects of the business, as Ted says he never knows what John will want to try next. Ted is pleased, however, that John is not as stubborn as he used to be. When he was sixteen, John wouldn't listen to anybody; now, however, Ted says that John may answer with a resounding "No," but he will at least listen to you. Herein lies an important realization: being a rock star is a corporate business; protecting and nurturing the corporate image—John himself—is a must. Coming to terms with this fact—as the family-run Mellencamp and Company is doing—is guaranteeing a shining future.

Amongst all of this corporate hype, however, John will remember his fans and that challenge and enjoyment are his motivations. This fun element will no longer be projected onstage through womanizing and profanity. This method has already been cooled down considerably, being replaced by high-level energy and intensified charisma. Once John brought a girl from the audience onstage with him. Later, her jealous boyfriend beat her up. The boyfriend took out his anger on the girl, not on John. Nevertheless, John felt badly once he learned about the incident and began to tone down the overt sexuality. This move will also broaden John's popular appeal, enlarging his arena of fans. Brown-haired and blue-eyed, John is a handsome man, yet he admits that he sometimes feels he is too old to have so many young girls as fans. But he does appreciate and acknowledge their loyalty. Onstage, John's moxie will replace sexuality. Onstage, John's panache will replace vulgarity. Offstage, John's apotheosis will widen his appeal, broaden his audience, sharpen his acumen, and solidify his star status. The force be with you, John!

As John copes with the obligations and responsibilities he encounters with fame and maturity, he does not forget about the laudable qualities so precious to youth. Mellencamp's uncanny ability to identify with both the ups and the downs that teenagers encounter is partly responsible for his populist appeal. Reflecting upon adolescence with a slight sense of melancholy, John identifies with teenagers, saying that each one of them wants to accomplish something, even though he or she has trouble defining exactly what he or she hopes to do. Seeing that he is also that way, John says he tries to capture these feelings in his songs. We all chase our dreams, which John thinks is important, as this process is what establishes our importance.

Openly and honestly, Mellencamp admits that he has had a chip on his shoulder. He sees teenagers as being in the same Catch-22 dilemma. All the teenagers desire, in Mellencamp's estimation, is to accomplish the same goal he upholds: to endure life and to survive intact. Adolescents are idealistic, but they need to understand how the world operates before they will be able to endure. Mellencamp sees trouble for any individual who allows his or her ideals to "cloud the reality." Ideals, nevertheless, are essential; without them, we become adults (like our parents) much too rapidly. As John warned in "Jack and Diane," teenagers must cling to being sixteen as long as possible, since changes will be arriving all too soon anyway.

Again, I applaud and respect Mellencamp's candidness, honesty, and new maturity. Media hypes have their place, of course, but they will no longer swallow John up. Promoters and executives will perform their duties, yet they will no longer have the nerve to prey upon John like a beast upon the flesh of an innocent lamb. Unfavorable reviews will exist, but John will learn how to accept them and internalize their critical content. His anger will give way to a businesslike pragmatism; after all, nobody can be *everything to everybody*. John candidly confesses, albeit, that unfavorable reviews anger him. Striving to be honest, trying to go that extra mile to make the interview successful, John sometimes feels "pissed off" when he responds directly and honestly to a serious inquiry. Agreeing or disagreeing with the interviewer, John is proud of the fact that he at least hasn't been sitting there "jacking you off."

Okay, sexual allusions aren't going to totally disappear from John's campy vocabulary. Nor is his sensitivity to his fans going to disappear. Once, in San Francisco, a biker tossed his leather jacket onto the stage, hitting John. The biker later told John that John was the first person who had been able to make him happy since Ronnie Van Zandt and the other members of Lynyrd Skynyrd went down in a plane crash. Moments like this create an empathy between a performer and his audience. Moments like this make all the hassles worth enduring. Moments like this also cue a rocker in, showing a singer the impact that he has on fans.

True, John's fighting, drinking, and loose living have driven the devil bowlegged; even his temper tantrums and his onstage performances have contributed to a controversial image that even John finds bothersome at times. John's mother, Marilyn, worries about his becoming a recluse as a result of his stardom. Or he could fall victim to the numerous other evils associated with the world or rock stars. But John's love of life—a basic theme in his lyrics—evokes a personal refusal to become another rock-and-roll casualty.

When I traveled to Seymour, I was lucky enough to visit one of John's cousins. This cousin possesses the insight to understand John. Speaking about a man/child that he both admires and respects, this cousin spoke about the now-famous rock star:

> When John was growing up, nobody understood him, except Grandma. Everybody was down on him. He wouldn't get a job. He was only interested in music, since age twelve. . . . His grandmother practically raised him. Once he made it, it didn't matter if he was an asshole. This success has changed John, too. Earlier, he was hard to get along with. He has changed now.
>
> I think success has been good for John Mellencamp. He has justified himself, his existence, in the eyes of his parents. . . . John is still very much a kid, but I've seen some good qualities come out in John over the recent past.[23]

Probing, I naturally asked this cousin to elaborate. He said that John is a spiritual person, although most people don't know this. He respects the devoutness of his grandmother and has been influenced by the Bible. Seeing life beyond the everyday, forty-hour–week, simpleminded stuff, according to this cousin, has taken John where he wanted to go. Isn't faith like this a basic concept of biblical teachings? John sent many demonstration tapes that were turned down because of their biblical allusions and connotations. So the cousin says that John became disgruntled and discouraged and ceased writing such songs. I hope John's maturity and self-understanding will allow him to return to this type of writing. John turns a good metaphor, and the Bible lends itself to metaphorical treatment.

Another aspect of John that is not so commonly known, except to family friends, according to this admiring cousin, is the impact that John's paternal grandfather had upon John's life. John dedicated both the *A Biography* album and the *Scarecrow* album to his grandfather. John has also related stories about how his uneducated Dutch grandfather never registered to vote because when he attempted to do so, the people laughed at his name: Harry Perry Mellencamp. Born on November 4, 1903, in Jackson County, Indiana, Harry was a strong-willed, determined, competitive fighter. His legacy, it seems to me, lives on in his acclaimed grandson, John Jay Mellencamp. Harry died on December 28, 1983, but he lived to see his beloved grandson carve an identity for himself. Harry and Laura are deserving of a part of the credit. Their encouragement, understanding, and love were constant sources of inspiration to John. Even when John was, in the eyes of others, trampling on their Nazarene convictions, John and his grandparents communicated with each other. Their commitment to John, like John's commitment to them and to his music, has delivered handsome dividends: financially, creatively, humanly, and, most important, spiritually.

Who is the guy, then, that John dislikes? First, John dislikes unreal images that emanate from the dreamland publicity machines of the industry. Perhaps he regrets outbursts like the ones that happened on CBS News Nightwatch and at London, Ontario. On the other hand, John sees these outbursts as being honest and real, even if they are infantile and costly.

Second, John has developed a distaste for what he sees as an infringement on his own style, and this has made him become condescending to people. This type of aloofness does not become him, even though the demands of fame and fortune sometimes dictate such treatment. While in Seymour, in August of 1984, I was surprised not to see a sign commemorating Seymour as the hometown of John Cougar Mellencamp. The mayor of Seymour, William W. Bailey, explained in a letter to me that he visited Marilyn, John's mother, "concerning the possibility of our community placing a sign at the east entrance of the city limits." Mayor Bailey thought that permission to do this should be granted, but he has never received any response. Is this foul-up a true result of fame and fortune or the undercurrent of a previous battle John had with a former mayor? Apparently, a former mayor battled with John about something relating to the *Chestnut Street Incident* album. Whatever this former mayor tried to do, John saw it as an infringement upon his style, or so it appears. But now John must dislike that aloof stubbornness that makes him unable to cooperate with a new mayor. I hope John's mellower nature will allow Seymour to recognize their most famous son.

Third, John must at least regret some of his past indulgences. All of us would like to return to our carefree youth and alter some of our mistakes. John has admitted that he hopes his three daughters excel scholastically at school, to at least accomplish more than he did. An adult always sees things differently than a kid. Even the rebel John sometimes sounds just like an authoritative teacher or parent. John must also hate (or at least regret) some of the identity-crisis problems he encountered. Fighting authority is one thing when a cause exists, but so much of John's fighting, swearing, drinking, and whoring served only to indulge his pleasure and boost his ego. His feelings of personal inferiority, which sometimes flare up today, must be overcome. They will be conquered, as his recent success is mellowing him. He has proven himself. His identity crisis and inferiority feelings caused his reckless behavior as a kid, as well as his substance abuse and his sexual exploits as a young man. Alcohol and dope are no longer part of his life. Also, he is exerting an effort to rectify his past transgressions. By all accounts, he is now a loyal husband and a devoted father. Maturity does offer some rewards! John does not seem quite so sophomoric or so vulnerable now that he has proven himself. Success allows us to stop trying to get even with God and the world. Even Mozart once said, "I've never been known for my overwhelming adultness." From one creative genius to another, John Mellencamp must know what Mozart meant!

Look at the words that have been used to describe John

Cougar/John Mellencamp. Not appearing in any particular order, just peruse the listing: *idiot, brat, bad boy, jerk, Little Bastard, fool, fast, stupid, insincere, imitative, obnoxious, rude, obsessive, impulsive, notorious, sophomoric, cocky, fiendish, rugged, ass, blue-collar, wild, untameable,* and *indifferent.* Indeed! What a collection! Just how can such a simple guy create so much animosity?

My prognosis has been that the image of John Cougar/John Mellencamp will undergo a total rebirth, a complete transformation. Once this process is completed, we should be witnessing a different list of words being used to describe this phenomenal star and unique personality. The new list will include such descriptive terms as: *tenacious, determined, persevering, resolute, charming, committed, admirable, noble, sensitive, intelligent, dedicated, religious, spiritual,* and *honest.*

Cast no doubts, however. John Cougar Mellencamp will endure the controversy, survive the competition, and enjoy long-term success. My hope is that he eventually drop "Cougar" and go with the name he prefers, John Mellencamp. Regardless, our hero from the Hoosier heartland will be entertaining us for years to come as singer, songwriter, producer, or talent scout. Too much of him is reflected within us; populism endures!

CHAPTER SIX

SON OF SEYMOUR

The Friday afternoon of August 17, 1984, was a typical end-of-the-week day. That Friday afternoon was also the first time I had ever been to Seymour, Indiana. The humidity was tolerable, the sun hot. Yet the air smelled clean and pure because a short summer shower had just fallen. It was no real thunderstorm, by any stretch of the imagination, merely a few drops to wetten the sidewalks and streets and put a fresh, clean scent into the somewhat balmy atmosphere.

I had taken I-69 into Indianapolis, then took I-65 south to Seymour. After checking in at the Best Western, I made my first of many journeys down Highway 50 into the downtown section. Closer to town, this highway becomes Tipton. When I hit Chestnut Street, a smile flooded my face. Chestnut Street was a landmark of sorts—at least for somebody researching Johnny Cougar. Here was the street immortalized on John's 1976 release, *Chestnut Street Incident*. A foreboding sense of anticipation, coupled with apprehension, hung over me as I headed north on Chestnut Street. What did I expect to find? I had never been here before. Maybe the rain was a spiritual symbol that Chestnut Street would speak to me, reveal the mysteries, and explain the fame. Chestnut Street could be Downtown Anywhere, at least anywhere in a small town in the Midwest.

But the significance of Cougar's use of the word *incident*

revealed itself eventually. Many people speak about the "incident"—some with pride, some with disgust. The "incident" has nothing to do with John Cougar himself, yet, as he was a high-schooler at the time, I'll wager that John Mellencamp was participating in the "incident." In John's day, which was actually not so frightfully long ago, since he graduated from Seymour High School in 1970, the "incident" was commonly referred to in the vernacular phrase of "scooping the loop." The first person to talk to me about this was a delightful lady who referred to it as the "kiddie parade that happens every Friday and Saturday." As I was an outsider, my beleaguered mind wondered what this lady was talking about. At first, I thought she meant an actual parade of children, maybe carrying their pet birds and dogs and snakes. But even Seymour, Indiana, wouldn't have a parade like this every Friday and Saturday. Then this lady said the "kiddie parade" wouldn't begin until around nine o'clock. My blank stare and bewildered expression must have led her to think I was pretty ignorant.

Then the moment of recognition arrived. Quite proud that I at least thought I knew what she was speaking about, I exclaimed, "You are talking about cruising, aren't you?"

"Yes," she responded, with deadpan humor, "that's what most people call it now."[1]

Call it cruising, scooping the loop, or Chestnut Street incident, the rose smells the same. The practice is becoming sort of a political problem. But, sure enough, on Friday and Saturday nights, a stream of cars drives up and down the famous lanes of Chestnut Street. Other cars, parked along the streets (diagonal parking is used in downtown Seymour), have teenagers sitting on the trunks, smoking cigarettes and passing the time. Some adults see nothing wrong with this scooping-the-loop practice on weekends. Others are outraged by the flagrant behavior of the kids. In all honesty, I was neither heckled nor harassed by these junior high and senior high students. But those opposed to the practice believe that I was lucky. Whether scooping the loop survives its brewing political confrontation or whether cruising dies an unnatural death, Chestnut Street will remain as the flamboyant symbol of an "incident" that makes (or made) teenagers feel powerful and allows them a certain degree of independence. John Mellencamp did not invent scooping the loop, but his anticipation generated a title for a record album and acted as the catalyst for his creative forces to compose a couple of songs for the album.

Of course, many towns (probably most towns) have cruising. But in Seymour, the practice seemed to be somewhat more institutionalized. This formalization, rather than the actual practice, is what surprised me. But another aspect of Seymour caught me off-guard. This time, the source of wonder was an omission, of sorts. Driving into any town, one sees a sign welcoming him to the town. More often than not, the sign gives the population of the city. Seymour is no exception, thus far. The sign is there. More often than not, either the Jaycees or the Lions (or both) erect some sign welcoming newcomers to the town. Once again, Seymour is no exception to this commonplace practice. In fact, a sign exists, telling everybody, "The Jaycees Welcome You to Seymour, Crossroads of Southern Indiana, Population 13,000." Okay, so the sign is a little outdated, not reflecting the most accurate population. It does, nevertheless, welcome folks to the city and boast a pride in the community.

What caught me unaware was the lack of any sign or of some public recognition of Seymour being the hometown of the rock phenomenon John Cougar Mellencamp. The acknowledgment need not be flashy or gaudy, but I did expect some attempt on the part of the community to make something out of the fact that a famous individual hailed from this conservative bastion nestled within the heartland of the country.

Several explanations for the absence of any sign were offered. One idea was that John had, to some degree, disassociated himself from Seymour, living in nearby Bloomington instead. This could be, perhaps, but a sense of the "what-came-first-the-chicken-or-the-egg" syndrome entered my mind. I did not argue with this person, but I had gathered the opinion that John left Seymour because Bloomington was more receptive to his concerts and more encouraging of his dreams. Who knows? Perhaps, suggested one person, since Seymour is a conservative community, some folks are somewhat embarrassed about the idea that a famous rock star—with all the negative connotations associated with rock—was raised in Seymour. If this is the case, John himself has done little if anything to arrest their embarrassment. Some of the statements John makes about himself and his school days certainly do play into the rebellious, wild image of a rock star.

Another explanation offered was that the city fathers and the mayor, now Bill Bailey, perhaps did not place any real significance on the fact that John is from Seymour. If this is the case, maybe they should think this through again! This is apparently not the case, however. I inquired, in a letter to Mr. Bailey, why no such sign existed, and Mayor Bailey responded. During the summer of 1983, Mayor Bailey visited with Marilyn, John's mother, concerning a sign at the east entrance to the city. Marilyn told Mr. Bailey she would see John that weekend and ask if John would grant permission for such a sign. As of September 4, 1984, the mayor says he has "not been contacted by any member of the family concerning this request."[2] Once again, Mellencamp's office has projected a negative public-relations image. If John were opposed to the sign, a simple "Thanks, but I am not interested" would at least not be rude. The request deserved a response, even if the answer was negative. Mayor Bailey says he is still interested in erecting a sign, but wonders if John and/or the Mellencamp family "may still harbour ill feelings as a result of some previous experience." John and a former mayor allegedly encountered some difficulty during the 1976 promotional blitz for the *Chestnut Street Incident* album. Nobody seems to recall whether the hassle involved the album's title or a song's lyrics. But Time's ticktock has apparently not yet healed John's anger; he must avoid *all* mayors!

We always say our close friends and our own family will serve as our harshest critics, no matter what the endeavor. This platitude lies at the core of the next explanation as to why Seymour has no sign recognizing John or why Seymour has not exploited the fact that John is from there. When *American Fool* was released, in 1982, local students wore John Cougar T-shirts, talked about his concert tour, and generated quite a stir of excitement. This is natural; *American Fool* sold well over 3 million copies, won two Grammy Awards, and won John some long-overdue recognition. This person implied that perhaps John has already peaked. After all, he reasoned, *Uh-huh* was not doing as well as *American Fool,* so the local hoopla died down a bit, since John appeared to be not as strong a force as he once was. Oh, yes, local critics and friends really are the most vindictive.

In my opinion, *Uh-huh* is better rock and roll than the *American Fool* album. Yet *Uh-huh* is not selling as successfully as *American Fool* did. *Uh-huh* is no failure, by any means. It has sold over 2 million copies, which is certainly successful, but *Uh-huh* is a different type of album. The songs reflect Mellencamp's style, rather than play into commercial salesmanship, as *American Fool* did. Each album, in essence, is trying to prove a different aspect of John's talent. He can generate a commercial success; now he has proven he can spin some true-grit rock and roll and make it a commercial success also. This is an achievement!

Any performer hopes to establish a stable position within the confines of the business. To Cougar and Company, this awesome responsibility has not yet been totally achieved. Attempts are directed at altering John's image. Overall, the drinking/fighting/balling image of the rebellious, conceited brat were just not convincing. As one travels on into his thirties, the image loses any appeal. Attending a John Cougar Mellencamp concert today and comparing it to a concert of several years back, one sees great differences. Now, John depends exclusively on his charismatic appeal, his musical genius, and his incredible energy to carry the show. He no longer relies upon a base vulgarity of crude language and aggressive remarks to win fans. He does not need to; I doubt that he ever did need to.

Stability and permanence are the names of the game. This is why the *Uh-huh* tour played to smaller audiences in smaller halls. Had Cougar and Company booked arenas and stadiums with a capacity of fifteen to twenty thousand seats, unsold tickets would have probably resulted in many locations. A shrewd and astute decision was made to book venues into smaller auditoriums, holding five to eight thousand fans. This way, the shows would sell out, leaving fans without tickets and creating more enthusiasm for the next tour. At the same time, the prestige of having a show be advertised as "sold out" perpetuates the concept/myth that all is perfect. But let's remember that a concert tour is a promotional tour. The real money and profits tumble in when the sales of the album increase, not so much from the tour itself. *Uh-huh* is an extraordinary album; don't misunderstand me. But, to book large arenas, selling twelve thousand seats and leaving six thousand empty seats is *not* as shrewd a business decision as booking smaller theaters and enjoying the "sold out" syndrome. Empty seats are contagious and should be avoided, particularly when they occur in large, highly visible numbers. And, as John says, he also feels closer to the audience in a smaller auditorium. This may be true, but until the permanence and stability of Cougar and Company are firmly established, such decisions as those made for the *Uh-huh* tour remain perceptive and astute.

Many variables enter into such a complex adventure as a rock-and-roll concert tour, just as many opinions exist as to why Seymour doesn't do more bragging about her favorite son. A local police officer, Richard Pennybaker, perhaps summarizes the feeling most palatably. Known as Rick to his friends, Officer Pennybaker told me that he and John were friends while in high school, although they ran around with different crowds. John was musical; Rick was athletic. But to Rick, his friendship with John is a friendship with a former buddy named John Mellencamp. Rick is not all that impressed with "Johnny Cougar." Thus, when he and John are together, they talk about old times, play football, and relate to each other as individuals. They avoid talking shop, so to speak, which creates the relaxing atmosphere of their visits. As Rick says, he and John were "not running buddies" in high school, but they see each other periodically. John, says Rick, is a high school friend; Rick cannot grasp the excitement people feel when they learn that he has been to John's house in Bloomington and that John has been to Rick's place also. Since John's friends and family know Rick and are used to seeing him around, Rick says he is sometimes asked by John to "keep an eye on him when he is in town—to keep people off him." When John was married to Vicki and when John's sister, Janet, was married, in 1984, Rick also served in this bodyguardlike capacity. Gatecrashers are a problem at times.[3]

Rick's perspective must be akin to that of many of the folks in Seymour. I had anticipated more bragging about John; but when you have known somebody all of his life, you do not need to brag about him. Folks are proud of John's phenomenal talents and his financial success, but they do not worship the ground he walks on. Rick's comments helped to clarify the phenomenon. And perhaps someday Seymour will acknowledge their pleasant industrial/farming community as the "Hometown of John Cougar Mellencamp." Let's hope so.

If Seymour waits too much longer, perhaps "Cougar" can be dropped. According to John, he was disgruntled and outraged when he first saw the *Chestnut Street Incident* album, which used "Johnny Cougar," the sexy and commercial title passed onto John from his first manager, Tony DeFries. Any fan is well aware of John's chagrin. But I suspect that John's anger emanates more from the authoritarian manner by which DeFries changed the name—without consulting John at all—than by the actual name itself. After all, being a "Cougar" is certainly nothing to be ashamed of. The cougar, a respected member of the cat family, is a large and powerful animal. The orangish/brown coloring provide it with beauty, as well. Cougars are also called catamounts or pumas. We can all agree that "John Cougar" certainly sounds better than "John Catamount" or "John Puma." Besides, the traits of the animal are admirable enough for the Ford Motor Division to manufacture a Mercury Cougar. So whether or not the "Cougar" name endures remains to be seen. Either way, the moniker possesses some intriguing implications for somebody such as John.

To be sure, John has never attempted to be any kind of dear. However, he has cooperated with the promulgation of a false image. As John's popularity stabilizes and solidifies, maybe the name "Cougar" eventually will be phased out. At that time, perhaps the false images can also die a natural death. These false impressions, perpetuated during the earlier days of his career, no longer serve John's best interests. John is thirty-four, an accomplished musician, a capable businessman, a dedicated parent, and a responsible adult. The sophomoric image of an irresponsible, self-indulgent, radical brat no longer enhances John's appeal. As a musician, he possesses the skill and the respect to allow his creative endeavors to rest upon their own popularity and universal appeal. As a person, he is "growing up, without giving in," as he says; he has learned to register his protest in a more productive manner than through anger and profanity. As a rock musician, he is part of a new wave of popular stars who are lucky enough to be able to flex their individual muscles, within limits, and be themselves onstage. Each individual is different; thus each individual rock performer must develop a show that capitalizes strengths and minimizes weaknesses. This is not tomfoolery; it is sound business. Like it or not, a successful rock band of this decade carries as much resemblance to a successful corporation as it does to the band that is still awaiting that first big break. John is intelligent, so these transitions will me made, the iconoclastic image alterations will occur, and perhaps the name "Cougar" will be dropped.

CHAPTER SEVEN

Chestnut Street Incident
Mainman/MCA, 1976

A twenty-five-year-old Johnny Cougar looks much younger than the present thirty-four-year-old man we identify as John Cougar Mellencamp. In fact, at first glance, many of us would not recognize this pompadoured kid as John Cougar at all. The cover of *Chestnut Street Incident,* Johnny Cougar's first album, produced by Tony DeFries, is the birth of the John Cougar Mellencamp we know today. Even though the cover pictures a clean-shaven, well-dressed young man, against a grayish background, the lyrics of Mellencamp's song still emote a love affair with the American dream, an attack on towns that stifle creativity and a tribute to perseverence and dedication.

On side 1, the opening song is called "American Dream." Written by John Cougar, the narrative deals with a young man's fear that the American dream is passing him by. Yet Cougar's poignant understanding of the underdog, coupled with his sympathy for the future faced by this guy and people like him, make "American Dream" a political statement, in a way. The American dream, as typified in stereotype, simply does not exist. John Mellencamp, at age twenty-five, was expressing his own feelings about the American dream. Hence "American Dream" is autobiographical.

The unifying theme of the lyrics revolves around an individual's quest for identity, search for recognition, and coming to terms with the ways of the world. Proudly, the speaker (Mellencamp?) admits that he is cute enough to impress the girls. However, when a winking eye and fancy clothes do not produce a female companion, he starts a fight. But, isn't that the American dream, he wonders? Yet the macho bravado is an act to conceal failure; what the speaker really seeks is the freedom to be what he wants. After all, he was raised on a strong dosage of self-reliance and the American way; nevertheless, learning that he could not be anything he wanted to be instilled a sense of betrayal, a feeling of being cheated out of his dream. Many of his buddies work at a local factory, Cummins, but he wanders aimlessly on the streets. Where is that elusive destiny? How does one actually live the American dream? In retrospect, of course, John Cougar Mellencamp has, indeed, lived the American dream. In 1976, however, when "American Dream" was written, Mellencamp was questioning the validity of what he had been told by adults, the value of one's own perseverance, and the meaning of the American dream itself.

I enjoy the song, not because it belongs up with the great rock-and-roll ballads of all time, but because it is honest and fair. Isn't it an image-breaker to hear Cougar using words like "dolled up" and "boyfriends"? The speaker—John Mellencamp himself, in my opinion—asks in each stanza if this life he is living is an embodiment of the American dream. (Cummins is a factory in Seymour that builds diesels, which indicates that John *is* writing autobiographically.) Any person can relate to this fear, regardless of age, gender, or background. The boy is scared. The boy has questions. The boy needs to talk to somebody. The boy fears for his future. This is life; it may be frightful, but it is life the way a naturalist might see it. What is the American dream? Will it touch him or pass him by? As adults, we can remember the feelings. As teens, we lived the feelings.

The next song that Cougar authored is titled "Dream Killin' Town." Again, the song appears to be somewhat autobiographical, as the chorus brings to mind a common Cougar theme. John himself was a dreamer, but how does a dreamer survive and endure in a town that seems determined to mold him into what society wants, killing and destroying his personal dreams in the process. Again, Mellencamp is attacking our social mentality of "you-got-to-get-right-with-the-program." The "town," in essence, is a symbol of society at large, of any "dream-killing" force.

As teenagers, don't we generally despise the towns we are reared in? They offer no excitement, no challenge, no future. Not until we are older, and have gained some maturity and lost some instability, are we able to see the positive aspects of our towns. John Cougar was a dreamer. He still is. Unfortunately, life and her reality are tough on a dreamer. Could John Cougar Mellencamp today be scared, even now that his dream has become a reality? Life has challenged young John, but it has also rewarded him. He may, at one time, have seen Seymour as a killer of dreams, but he certainly doesn't see his home that way now. Concepts change. People change. Cougar changed.

Another poke at small towns is "Chestnut Street Incident," the title song of the album. Small towns, to the young protagonist, seem to have tied his hands, denied his independence, compromised his hopes, and smashed his dreams. Lyrics such as this might be a partial explanation of why John's hometown of Seymour, Indiana, seemingly lacks pride in what John Mellencamp has accomplished in the competitive arena or rock. Mellencamp, or whomever the speaker might be, sees himself as a prisoner of his small town, working from nine to five and wondering why everything turns out differently than originally planned. The only claim to fame is the attention he usurps vicariously, as a result of comparing his "sleek young silhouette" to the precision performance of a Corvette Sting Ray. His salvation, he realizes, is superficial, yet he prays to God that he will be able to hang onto the romantic fantasy that conceals his pain—at least to the outside world, if not to his own inner psyche. This small-town kid may be "used like a toy," but he continues to nurture the hope that fame and fortune will someday dock at his port.

The lyrics here *have* to be autobiographical! The small-town environment, being disbelieved when telling people he was going to make a record, knowing both winners and sinners, hanging out on the corner, and working dead-end jobs all spell out "This is my life." But the speaker here is wiser than the speaker in "American Dream." Here the metaphors are better: "this house of detention" is more effective than "those stories would choke a semi." "Chestnut Street Incident" enjoys a more refined poetic form, with its alliteration and symbolism, also. Interestingly enough, John Cougar Mellencamp today owns a 1963 Corvette Sting Ray, a symbol of success that he does keep in perspective. (A friend of John's told me that this Sting Ray is being traded for a tennis court at John's house.) But didn't we all see the Sting Ray as a symbol of earthly perfection? Also interesting is the fact that Mellencamp was wailing about being an innocent small-town kid that is used before he was totally through with his dealings with Tony DeFries, his first manager. And, yes, John Cougar manages to "blow us away" with some of his statements and behavior, But we accept him as he was and as he is; walking around in his shoes makes these statements and actions more palatable.

The flip side of the album has a similar song, titled "Chestnut Street Revisited." Many of the stanzas are either identical or nearly so, but they reveal more of John Cougar's inner soul. He worked hard through high school, then formed his own rock band. But the constant work, the meager wages, the unanswered questions, and the hard-to-define dream robbed him of his fun. The ridicule was tolerated, however; nursing a dream that appeared beyond reach was a source of fulfillment, of self-esteem. Even back in 1976, young John lived on a day-to-day basis, blocking out the preachings of those who claimed his dream was unreal.

Like Mellencamp himself, this vulnerable speaker is vying for his individual identity in a mass society that expects conformity from the individual, yet carelessly ignores the individual. But even then, like Mellencamp says, his band helps him keep his head on straight. But hard work and little pay did not defeat the boy and his band. The speaker also learns he cannot be everything to everybody. He cannot make everybody happy all the time. But once he discovers his dream—and we all possess dreams—he will be better prepared to understand and to cope with reality. But until the speaker discovers his identity, reality is a threat to be evaded. The band will help him achieve an identity, a permanence, and a happiness! Nice going, John. You stuck it out. You won.

The other songs on the album include two less revealing songs written by Cougar and five cover songs. Written by Cougar, "Good Girls" is a satirical treatment honing in on girls with the good reputations who, in reality, are not everything they seem to be. The chorus, however, relishes in sexual suggestion. The speaker, critically rejecting their careless fakery and their shallow deportment, refuses to walk and talk with these frauds. He is willing to meet them at night, however. Lust and sexual gratification do not require him to respect them, only to indulge in his pleasure principle. All of us, at times, find ourselves in situations where our genitals are doing our thinking for us. The song is not bad, but Cougar is strongest when he develops more of a ballad-type narrative. "Sad Lady," another song he wrote for the album, suffers in its lack of hope. Cougar is at heart an optimist, with naturalistic tendencies. "Sad Lady" is a depressing song. The lady curses her name, is ashamed, feels she was born in vain, and has nobody to blame for her desperate dislike of and revulsion for life. This is the only song of Cougar's where I see a glorification of the death wish. This lady is so without hope that she will continue to wish for death. And, says Cougar, whenever life itself is so miserable, dying does not seem bad. The Sad Lady is so misunderstood that even Cougar cannot offer any hope and solace. This is not Cougar at his best.

The five cover songs included on the album are a decent rendition of Roy Orbison's "Pretty Woman"; a cover of Elvis Presley's "Jailhouse Rock"; a song called "Supergirl" and another called "Do You Believe in Magic?"; and the Doors' "Twentieth Century Fox." Generally, Mellencamp feels more at home with his own songs and projects a better symbiotic relationship between the artist and the song. I enjoy his "Jailhouse Rock," but can anybody do that song better than the King?

Who can really say why *Chestnut Street Incident* didn't enjoy any commercial success when it was released in England in 1976? Maybe too many cover songs. Maybe inadequate promotionals. Maybe not enough radio time. Maybe the songs are no good. But *Chestnut Street Incident* was not a real flop. Today it is a real find in a record-bin sale, if you are lucky! Six weeks and twenty dollars located me a copy through a record-finding service.

About midsummer of 1984, the *Chestnut Street Incident* album became readily available, but not with the original cover of the cute "Johnny Cougar." This new release had a cover that uses the name "John Cougar Mellencamp" and pictured a sexy, shirtless John. Several pictures on the reverse side of the album jacket also reveal a bare-chested star; the cover picture, I am told, was never liked by John. It was originally intended to be used on a poster. The back side of the album jacket also has news clippings which contain false information. For example, one article mention's John's "unexpected marriage in his senior year of high school and the birth of a son two years later." True, John's marriage to Priscilla occurred while John was still in high school, but the child—a girl—arrived a little more than six months after the marriage, not two years later. Even today, as far as I can determine, John has fathered no sons.

CHAPTER EIGHT

The Kid Inside
Mainman/MCA

(Recorded circa 1977, Released 1984)

Against a yellow background, the cover of *The Kid Inside* pictures androgynous "John Cougar" dressed in what appears to be a blue bathrobe, with a red towel draped around his neck. The album was co-produced by Mainman and John himself, but it was never released. During 1984, this album suddenly and mysteriously began to show up in record stores. Tony DeFries seemingly wanted to "cash in" on the sensational popularity of his one-time protégé, so he made the arrangements to release the album for a first run on the market. Avoiding a direct assault on what DeFries did, John does have an opinion about the release of *The Kid Inside:* "He suffered the repercussions, not me. If he'd have been smart about it, he'd have worked with us, because I've got other records that never came out in America. We could've put together a compilation. But it was the way he did it. He released it right on the tail of *American Fool*, and it confused a lot of people."[1] From a businessman's viewpoint, DeFries was shrewd. His former protégé had a platinum album and two Grammy Awards, so DeFries's timing was geared to literally capitalize on that situation. DeFries, however, had nothing directly to do with creating the situation. Fans were somewhat bewildered. Suddenly two Cougar albums had appeared on the market. "What is John trying to do to us? Bleed our wallets?" was the reaction. But, as is not uncommon in the business, an unknown singer with "hungry" hopes will sign away the rights to the songs on the early albums. As we know, a struggling musician might sign almost anything in order to clinch the record deal. From the viewpoint of directness and honesty, however, Tony DeFries's actions were just one more snub of John and of what he represents. To me, though, Cougar's statement about what Tony DeFries did was an invitation to bury the hatchet, to reconcile their differences, and to at least work in harmony when circumstances so required. Legally, DeFries would be under no obligation to consult John about the release of the album. Thus the appearance of the album was probably as much of a surprise to John as it was to his loyal fans. In April of 1984, I bought *The Kid Inside* for $5.97, thinking I had discovered a great find. In July, the same store was selling the tapes in a special bin for ninety-nine cents.

The opening song on the album, appropriately enough, is titled "The Kid Inside." To those of us who see maturation in John Cougar Mellencamp today, the opening verses become significantly relevant and typically Cougaresque. Face pressed to the window, fingers running through his hair, Cougar's protagonist comes to the realization (albeit a haunting one) that only he really cares about what happens to him. Even his lady—whom he desperately needs to count on for support in this circular whirlwind we call life—says negative things about him. Is she shielding her own vulnerable pride, he wonders. Painfully candid, the lad admits that the hurt has opened his wounds and revealed his pain. How many times can "the kid inside" be killed? When does the kid strike back, with a choking hold on the throat? We can only hope violent retaliation will be avoided, but the frightened and intimidated adolescent fears that he is reaching the limit: the kid inside deserves to be freed, if he is to survive at all.

The speaker, needless to say, is a young, confused kid looking for compassion, understanding, and identity. To bet on whether or not Cougar is speaking about himself, my money goes on "win." The search for identity—Who am I? What am I doing here?—is a basic theme common to many of Cougar's songs, the popular smash hits as well as the obscure, ignored should-have-been–hits. Typical of kids, the speaker probably exaggerates when he says that "nobody cares but me." His parents care, yet these are the hurting years of adolescence when parents and their values do not count. Mellencamp uses the word *madness* to describe the loss of identity he suffers when he does begin to get close to the girl, when they do begin to think alike. Cougar has hit upon a basic complexity in our psychological make up. We want closeness, yet it terrifies us. We want closeness, yet we don't know how to accept it when it is offered. We want closeness, yet we want independence. How is a proper balance discovered? This dilemma makes the thought of falling in love a fearful one.

The strength of this opening song is another basic trait of Cougar's songs: the central character is confronting a dilemma we all face. Cougar's winners and his losers are like us; his songs strike a universal commonality within us all. Cougar possesses an uncanny inner sense of existential singularity. This basic essence of humanity that makes us all "one" is seen in the rest of Cougar's song also.

As "The Kid Inside" continues, the speaker observes that this girl laughs at things that are painful to him. He wonders if this is how she conceals her own feelings of inadequacy. He says she always belittles somebody (usually him) in order to make herself feel taller (possessing greater self-esteem). Then, since this reaction is increasing in its frequency, he reveals the additional frustration he encounters when he is likened to Mr. Springsteen. How will he ever justify himself when nobody bothers to support and/or to listen to him?

This direct reference to Bruce Springsteen is interesting. Through no fault of Bruce's, John has always been compared to

Springsteen. John has urged critics not to compare newcomers to him. Don't do to some newcomer what was unintentionally done to him, saddle him with a monkey on his back, is his unspoken plea. Cougar admonishes critics to realize that the newcomers he is compared to will be somewhat contemptuous of him, just as he felt contempt toward Springsteen. Says Cougar: "Here's the deal. When Dylan started, everybody compared him to Woody Guthrie and then Springsteen came along, and he was a fucking Dylan clone. And then I came along, and I'm a Springsteen clone. But the bottom line is, it all started with Woody Guthrie, and I'll be damned if 'Hurts So Good' sounds like 'This Land Is Your Land.' "[2] True to form, Cougar responds to and answers his critics. Yet, also true to form, Cougar avoids direct criticism of a fellow musician. He realizes the problem is not the fault of Bruce Springsteen himself, so he shows a professionalism and a humanitarian maturity in dealing with the frustrating comparison.

After the reference to Springsteen, the chorus intervenes, then a final verse concludes the song. This last verse is saturated with another basic theme of Cougar's songs: adapting to the circumstances that exist, so as to insure survival. In this final verse, Mellencamp cries to his listeners to understand that he would rather be himself than anybody else, dead or alive. A fighter, Mellencamp knows he will ultimately be a winner. When the chips ae really down, Mellencamp still has the intestinal fortitude not to give up on himself, not to sacrifice his dream. The song ends with the speaker heeding the listener with a moral: Believe only in what you can see. When the instrumentals silence themselves, one of The Zone members is heard to utter, "Ha-ha-ha, we'll keep it." Simple pride. Simple satisfaction.

With the opening line of "Take What You Want," the next cut, Cougar coaxes us to put our lives and our money up front, for all to see. The moral of believing only in what you see is repeated here. The second and last verst best conveys the alienation theme, as the singer enjoys sex without commitment, but also without meaning. The aimlessness, the searching, the emptiness are all conveyed in Cougar's narrative lyrics. After the couple indulge their sexual appetites, the man sees no reason to stay around talking, as he is an inept conversationalist. Besides, he then informs her that he is leaving town the next morning. Obviously, the intensity of their sexuality has not climaxed in a meaningful relationship. Void of commitment, meaning, and love, life is empty and meaningless.

"Cheap Shot" is next, reflecting the same search for acceptance, happiness, and identity. Out cruisin' the town, the speaker is looking for somebody to fight. Then he picks up his girl, takes her to a triple-X, and rubs his hand across her dress. The song concludes by his challenging the reader to take other cheap shots, not to be a candy ass, because everybody enjoys taking a cheap shot; doing so is such fun. The term "cheap shot" refers to any self-indulgent, socially unapproved behavior that provides the speaker with a thrill without offering any of the permanence and contentment the speaker needs. The speaker even implies that the "cheap shots" are somewhat degrading, on a human level, but what else does life offer?

A slower tempo ushers in "Sidewalks and Streetlights," a moody ballad with piano interludes and slurred vocals. Autobiographically, young Cougar is literally facing a personal struggle with the record-company personnel, with Tony DeFries and the name change, and with the possibility of fame and wealth. No matter what, life seems to conjure up difficulties. The power structure promises the young initiate stardom, so he assumes that he should "go for it." Having his name changed seems like a small price to pay, yet he is nonplussed over the finesse that the promoters use in their threatening maneuvers.

Stardom and fame have been the objective, yet when promised by somebody, they become threatening. How absurd! How unfair! But even though the game—be it stardom or life in general—is threatening, we are obligated to play. The thoughts continue to sporadically flash through the speaker's mind, with little congruity and little solace. The sidewalks and streetlights create a comforting and restful backdrop for all the confusion that is culminating in so much inner turmoil. The protagonist even questions his own priorities: Is being famous so important? Does he yearn for stardom because of the glory, or does he want fame because of the money? Either way, the danger and the risks are frightening. But he decides to play the game, as he is playing to win and he is playing for keeps.

Obsession seems to drive the speaker—Cougar himself—into playing the game, even though he is uncertain about what he even wants the outcome to be. Does he want to be a star? He thinks so. Today, John Cougar Mellencamp denies that he is a "rock star," as that is some image he has never wanted to achieve. Does the speaker in the song want glory, fame, and money? He thinks so. But he isn't sure how he'll cope with these things. Life without them he knows; life with them presents a threatening unknown. Such is life, we all learn, sooner or later.

Side 1 concludes with a light, sophomoric tune called "R. Gang." The "R" means "our." The song deals with the significance of friends, as the bunch of boys functions as a support group that will listen to him when others dish out their ridicule. Later, Cougar satisfactorily reveals that he is proud to have this bunch of boys to run with Saturday nights. A typical "yea for the night out with the guys" song, it does, nevertheless, reveal that John Cougar is, indeed, human: he writes insightful, autobiographical songs with universal themes and human relevance; he also writes superficial, fun songs that are void of deeper meanings and symbolic themes.

Side 2, opening with "American Son," is strong, direct, and revealing. The chorus rings with the confession that the speaker sees himself as the American Son, dreaming of becoming number one. Mellencamp's tinge of romantic wanderlust is present, as he enjoys being one of the last of the American Sons.

Cougar lurches for that universal heartstring again, knowing that we all have fantasies about being best in our field, whatever the field happens to be. He also perpetuates his James Dean–type battle to consistently be competing for approval from Dad. He doesn't want the Father to reject him, nor does he want to be ignored by the Father. John Mellencamp, like James Dean, yearns to live up to the father's exhortations, to win approval and acceptance.

As a high school teacher, I find a later verse intriguing. Cougar projects the image of his being a boozer and a fighter while in high school, yet witness what he acknowledges: fools are generally known to be self-indulgent, believing that an education is something they do not need. Surprisingly, Mellencamp lambasts these fools for destroying anything they fail to comprehend and for shooting down any self-concept that they have failed to live up to. Ultimately, the dealer (reality) grabs these fools by the genitals (to guarantee their undivided attention) and instructs them about the ways of the world.

How autobiographical can a writer be? How self-revealing can a writer be? How candidly honest can a writer be? I applaud this type of writing, even with its vivid, vulgar (painful?) imagery, as it reminds me of Mark Twain. Twain used to say that when he was ten, he was appalled at how ignorant and ill advised his father was. By the time Twain hit twenty, he felt his father was coming around, to some extent, and was at least a little better attuned to life. But when another decade passed, with Twain at thirty, he was astonished at how intelligent his father had become in such a brief span of time. How had his father learned so much so fast? Kids age, gaining maturity, gaining confidence, and reevaluating fathers.

The words are also interesting from the standpoint of John's performance while at school in Seymour. Whatever scholastic talents John possessed, they were well concealed. He regretfully recalls:

> In high school they had honor rolls. To make the honor roll you had to make sixteen points. We had our own honor roll. If you make one point, you made our honor roll. I'd walk out of high school and have three F's, two D's and a C. That was the highest score any of us had. We sort of tried to get the worst grades. It was rebellion. I hope my kids don't do anything this dumb.[3]

Admitting that one is wrong requires maturity, gracefulness, confidence, and security. As a teacher, I also hope that John's three daughters are wiser than their father. I wonder how hard one has to try to score low?

"American Son" even possesses a title that tears at the soul of our universal kindred spirit. The song, running just short of five minutes, is a serious, yet fun, account of how a young boy endures adolescent fantasy and ultimately grows up without necessarily giving in. He does, after all, learn that everybody is not what they appear to be and that he must be responsible for himself. But this is the land of opportunity and he is the "American Son."

"Gearhead" lacks the dynamic force of "American Son," but it is a haunting and moody number. Here Cougar advises us to stifle our tendency to talk and instead claim that we were only teasing. Do his confidence and his mouthiness cause some trouble? Cougar admits that they do. With an aura of defiance, the chorus reminds us that we are never alone, because the competition spits into your faces. John craves vivid images! This is not a great song, nor is it particularly memorable, but it is another example of Cougar expresing his opinions and observations through his music.

The light, happy piano interludes within "Young Genocides" prove to be a contrast to the heavy, disturbing content of the lyrics. Like John Cougar Mellencamp himself, "Young Genocides" is short, powerful, and forceful and gnaws at our understanding of what we are and what we dream of being.

Fate (Destiny) intervenes in the lives of the young genocides, those whose zombielike existence has hidden whatever success they have experienced. Blank stares cover their faces, as thoughts of fratricide infilter their minds. Feeling unimportant, being backed into the proverbial corner, the genocides live a life of impossible illusions parading around as Tomorrow. Again, Mellencamp bombards us with conflicting images, yet he drives his point home. The brief walk through the mind of John Cougar Mellencamp ends on a note of optimism!

The personification of Destiny; the metaphor of being trapped, with one's back to the wall, with no escape; and the metaphorical treatment of Tomorrow are all useful and functional poetic devices. But hope springs eternal: the suicides did not actually kill themselves. They only contemplate death as an escape, they don't use it. Success is disguised, not unexistent, and Tomorrow is a symbol of a better day!

The next song, "Too Young to Live," has a scary twist in its title. Being "too young to die" would be understandable; the reverse is frightening. The James Deanian conflict between father and son is here, and the Cougaresque themes of fear, escape, pressure, and insecurity also drop in. "Too Young to Live" runs for nearly eight minutes, yet it does acknowledge that, even with parental pressures and conflicts, one's family can also be one's refuge and his salvation. Toward the end of the song, Cougar rejects the advice that comes from his father, choosing to remember his mother's adage about the family being one's best friend, over the long haul. The speaker cries at night, hoping for somebody to help him along. The speaker thinks about suicide, with the purchase of a six-pack of beer. But these thoughts are not a death wish; most of us comtemplate suicide, even if merely out of idle curiosity. Part of the chorus says that though someone may act like nothing matters and live dangerously, sometimes he or she does survive. The title that grabbed us is now clarified: the song does not glorify death; it does not advocate the termination of life.

The opening stanza is typical Mellencamp in that it creates a vivid image that we all have experienced. High school students—such as John himself—concentrate on being cool and cope with being "jacked around" by fathers who tell them what to do, force their opinions onto them, and make them feel like clowns. Their mothers demand to know when they will return home each evening. So the browbeaten lad leaves the house because he cannot tolerate any more of this intimidation and must try to clarify his own moral code of right and wrong.

Don't blow this out of proportion. We do not have a psychopathically troubled teenager here. We have a common domestic confrontation between the quest for teenage independence, trust, and freedom, with the demand of parental authority and concern. The kid is angry, to be sure, but he is not dangerous. Look at John Cougar Mellencamp. Was he dangerous? Was he psychopathically maladjusted or unstable? Of course not. He was a typical teenager who argued with his folks and had a typical inner conflict between seeking his father's approval and fighting his father's competitiveness.

Following "Too Young to Live" is a related song, strongly similar in its theme of searching for security and acceptance. Together, both of these related songs run nearly twelve minutes. This one even carries one of Mellencamp's themes as its title. The name of the song is "Survive."

Who knows how to survive better than John? No matter, though; he doesn't quit. He holds out hope for finding a girl with devotion, commitment, and love. The internal rhyme *(devotion/ocean)* is cleverly effective, with its smooth sound, but the sexual images are also effective.

Once one admits that his level of tolerance has been reached, he realizes that many others have an attitude problem and cannot attune themselves to their own feelings. So Mellencamp advises these comrades to steal somebody else's ideas as their own, using self-masturbation as the tool of adoption. Mellencamp has a problem telling somebody what to do, yet he says that he has "scratched off a time or two," testifying to the validity of the process. To write about straightening out one's thinking through a combined process of both physical and mental masturbation is symbolic, vivid, intriguing, and true to life. Only speculation can surmise how autobiographical this revelation is for John Mellencamp himself, but, nevertheless, John shows an insight into the blurring of the fine line between fantasy and reality. He also emotes a keen understanding of and sympathy for people.

The last stanza is less metaphorical, but it seems to confess to a sense of narcissism. Now beware of faulting John for this. Psychologically, a balanced sense of narcissism is essential to a stable personality. After all, he who hates himself is not a socially adjusted individual. If one cannot love and accept himself, how does he expect anybody else to? But the "love song" concept mentioned toward the end is actually a reference to John's quest for self-esteem and self-understanding. The love song, Cougar says, is written in order for him to survive. Whenever he is seen walking down the street, he wants this friend to acknowledge how fine he looks. Even if the compliment is insincere, the comment will help them break the ice. Survival, alas, necessitates a degree of narcissism; without this, self-acceptance and self-realization will never materialize. What a vicious, ironic cycle.

Mellencamp claims that rock-and-roll music allowed him to pull his act together. Here he seems to be conveying this idea in song: the writing of "Survive" allows him the psychological outlet, the emotional pressure valve that he requires. Writing and singing—John's ways of releasing his feelings and expressing his opinions—are John's salvation and redemption. They give him life. They give him compassion. They give him understanding. They give him identity.

Reminiscent of the "hanging onto sixteen" in his blockbuster hit "Jack and Diane," John's chorus in "Survive" serves as an earlier affirmation of a similar thought. The chorus encourages us to survive, to stay alive, to forget about being sixteen or even twenty-five again.

Again John Cougar Mellencamp celebrates the meaning and significance of life, even when we are being dealt a losing hand. This love of life also surfaces in "Authority Song," a recent hit, when he says that maturity requires us to grow older, moving closer to death. To John, death doesn't sound like much fun, even though life constantly threatens survival. Adolescents generally fear maturation and its inherent responsibilities and obligations. But as John Mellencamp so succinctly and logically points out, the alternative is not overly comforting. Jack and Diane did the best that they knew how. John Mellencamp admires them for this. John Mellencamp does the best that he knows how. John Mellencamp wants everybody to keep fighting, so as to do the best that they can. Life is a game, a fight, a struggle. But the rewards are there.

Overall, *The Kid Inside,* as an album consisting of ten songs, is a valid representation of John Mellencamp's talent. And, in sale bins around the nation, it certainly is, in my humble opinion, a glorious discovery. Tony DeFries, one is safe to assume, released *The Kid Inside* on the heels of *American Fool* in order to cash in on Mellencamp's widespread appeal and growing popularity. His intent was probably financial gratification, not professional courtesy to John. However, perhaps fans of John's will purchase the album. True, they'll contribute to the coffers of Tony DeFries, but they'll also hear and sense a younger, less mature, less directed John Cougar sing his heart out to them. Maybe, over the long haul, the greed of Tony DeFries will actually enhance John Mellencamp's standing in the rock-and-roll game. *The Kid Inside* offers fans an additional opportunity to travel down the runway of John Cougar Mellencamp's mind. For my money, this is a golden opportunity, even though all ten of the songs are not great!

CHAPTER NINE

A Biography
Riva, 1978

On this album, John's band is referred to as Streethart. Like John himself, methinks the band might also have an identity crisis. Nevertheless, the album—which is difficult to acquire because it was never released in the United States—consists of ten songs written solely by John. The album also is a bargain because it plays for nearly forty-three minutes! But these are only two of the unique qualities of this album. John dedicated this album to his grandfather, an individual who played a strong role in shaping John's personality and molding John's destiny. This paternal grandfather, Harry Mellencamp, died on December 28, 1983, but he did live long enough to see his loving grandson become a respected, acknowledged singer and songwriter.

Due to the stereotypes we commonly hold of John, the consumer is not surprised to see that the opening number is titled "Born Reckless." The chorus is simple enough. The title is repeated three times, followed by the introduction of the concept that the speaker will remain reckless until he dies. The remaining lyrics, however, are earlier examples of John's struggle for identity, his desire to mature, and his need for understanding. One of the strengths of John's writing is its favorable blend of universality and simplicity. One can speculate and conclude that John is speaking about himself here. The lyrics certainly sound like

John talking, and if so, John has no reason to be ashamed or embarrassed. On the other hand, if one does not like autobiographical interpretations, the universality of John's songs allows the speaker to be anybody. Straightforwardly, this speaker admits that he has not grown up yet and that his attempts to do so have proven difficult.

These lyrics certainly nourish our concept of John; he was twenty-six when *A Biography* was released. Indeed, considerable growing up has occurred over the past eight years. The second stanza is even more Cougaresque. This stanza, my favorite of the three, unifies the song and serves as a transitional pivot upon which to progress to the climax. Now the speaker says he has been pushed around, even though he has had some opportunities to do some pushing himself. Overall, however, he decides that he deserved the rough treatment that flowed his way. At last, this Cougaresque antihero praises his friend who holds his hand when the real world has struck him down. Although he doesn't understand how he and this friend found each other, he is eternally grateful that they did.

To me, these are superb lyrics—simple, poetic, understandable, meaningful, and memorable. As is typical of Cougar's lyrics, the vocabulary is down to earth and direct. The alliteration of the "s" sound, the repetition of key words, and the somewhat inconsistent rhyme scheme do incorporate basic poetic techniques that add to the *sound* of the song. These same techniques also enhance our comprehension of what is being said. Because all of us have felt pushed, ignored, and wronged, we are able to sympathize and identify with the speaker—be it John or Anybody; perhaps "Hand to Hold On To" was being conceived when this song was written.

The speaker in the final verse pays tribute to the enduring love and compassion his girl has held for him. No matter what he did to her or how badly he treated her, she continued with her undying love for him. And even though he has not always deserved this support, he has appreciated it and is pleased (and surprised) that she has stayed with him. This scenario, of course, rests on the assumption that the speaker is a male and that the other person is a female. No tricky assumptions thus far, right? One wonders, if we interpret autobiographically, if the speaker is John and the woman is Priscilla, his first wife. Although the marriage ended in divorce in 1981, John had been married to Cil (as she is called) since May of 1970, a few weeks prior to his graduation from high school. Again, maybe an autobiographical interpretation is misleading, but one often writes about his feelings and these emotions would certainly seem to enter into John's personal life at the time. John's dedication to music would place a strain on any marriage, as would the responsibility of raising a child and holding a job. This final stanza is a poignant "thank you" to this strong lady who had endured so many trials. The speaker even experiences difficulty arranging his words and expressing his thoughts. Aren't we all—including John himself—like this?

Stumbling for the correct words, the protagonist confesses that he has lied and cheated and lacked compassion for this true friend. Even so, this antihero hopes that she will stay with him. Unsure of himself and ashamed of his behavior, he is surprised that she has not hit the road already, as he has been so egotistical and self-centered. Although he has taken whatever he needed from her, he wants her to know that nobody is waiting in the wings to replace her. Their love has been unstable, but in his own selfish manner, he loves her still.

The speaker sounds as though he is afraid to love. But at this time, the marriage of John and Cil was a struggling one. Not an unusual predicament, to be sure, but like "Jack and Diane" of future fame, John and Cil did the best they could. But, like Jack and Diane, their best proved not to be good enough. The marriage failed in 1981, after nearly eleven years and one daughter. A younger lover, named Vicki, took Cil's place.

Turning away from the domestic life, the next entry, called "Factory," deals with blue-collar, dead-end jobs that offer no meaningful challenges. All the speaker yearns for is the five o'clock whistle. Working at the factory is the name of the game, however, as it provides the resources that are necessary to "cruise the scene" and hustle the ladies. Using one eye to watch the time clock and the other eye to watch the girl in the hallway, the speaker's anticipation for the evening's attractions heightens in intensity. Then, near the end of the song, the protagonist realizes that the rising sun will begin the routine anew: he will return to the futureless factory, dream about the after-hours entertainment, and ignore the feelings of being caught in a trap. Mellencamp wants us to feel sorry for this individual. But our sympathy is a two-edged sword: we feel badly that he receives so little fulfillment in life; we also feel irritated that he lacks the drive and the initiative to accept responsibility for himself and to alter his destiny. True, the factory is a prison of lost hopes, but he must shoulder a chunk of the blame for this dilemma.

"Night Slumming" continues in a similar vein, although it runs much longer, over four and a half minutes. Concluding this song is a "Stension Chorus," sung by some twenty people: Streethart, the band; John's wife, Cil, and his daughter, Michelle; and a dozen or so others. The lyrics of the tune illustrate various aspects of this offbeat nightlife that is being described. In addition to brothels and prostitutes, we have homosexuals. The narrator, asserting his straight sexuality, says he is not a king, but he is not a princess either. In other words, he is not perfect, but he is not gay. In the same sentence, he claims that he does not drink himself into a stupor, as there are other ways to be blown away. This sexual imagery, albeit vivid and graphic, is consistent with the offbeat nature of the lyrics. This guy also seems proud of his claim that he sleeps all day, making work impossible. Sadly, though, we learn that anything he saw as positive has been lost to him. The only symbol of hope for this forlorn figure is his girl, whose love he hangs onto. But "night slumming" apparently serves as the pinnacle of his dreary, futureless, hopeless existence. John's naturalism and environmental determinism creep in here. But so does a social statement of sorts: maybe no one person or no one institution is responsible for these night slummers' being there, but the shameful waste of human potential is a disgrace nevertheless.

The fourth song on side 1 is a favorite of mine. "Taxi Dancer" shows young Mellencamp at his best. More than most people,

John believes in his own dreams and is willing to concentrate his efforts and pay the price to see his dreams blossom into reality. This album, *A Biography*, was released in England; this version of "Taxi Dancer" that appears here is slightly different in tone than the version we are more accustomed to, on the *John Cougar* album. Here the pace sways, the tempo slows, and the voice becomes gravely, albeit sexually. The guitar accompaniment even seems a little more prominent in this version, which is a little shorter than the *John Cougar* rendition of 1979. The lyrics are unchanged; the shortness of the 1978 arrangement is the result of not singing the chorus after the first verse. Thus the chorus is only heard twice, instead of thrice, as in the version we in the United States are more familiar with.

In "Taxi Dancer," the contradictions of desperation and of hope confront us. Also, the narrator's empathy for the dancer is both encouraging and devastating. Cougar is strong on having dreams, as they instill us with hope, the courage to venture on with life. And, as we would anticipate, whenever these dreams are squashed by the realities of life, Cougar feels real pain, real anger, and real sorrow. But, being mortal, what can he do, other than hold her close, dance with her, listen to her, and cry for her?

This ambitious young lady dreamed of becoming a professional dancer on the Broadway stage. So she left Pasaroba to go to the Big Apple: the town of romantic dreams, but also the city of dashed hopes. A small-town girl unaccustomed to city life, she was forced to accept a job as a maid at the Grammercy Park Hotel. Audition after audition gave her only defeat, so she started dancing at a New York bar, trying to survive on her own. In the last verse, the sympathetic and compassionate narrator says that he has lost track of the Taxi Dancer, but the last he heard, she frequents a bar on Forty-second Street, where she drowns her anguish in beer and sits alone, defeated by the natural forces in the real world. The final image is shocking, yet fitting. In this bar, the Taxi Dancer sometimes dances with an old butch who shoves a quarter into the jukebox. Dancing with a butch, for free, certainly is not the dream that the Taxi Dancer nurtured when she left Pasaroba. But, as the thrice-repeated chorus tells us, the narrator will hold her close, listening to her tale of outgrown dreams while they pretend that the dance floor in this crummy bar is a Broadway stage. Even in utter defeat, a tinge of the dream lives on!

Amen for the poignancy and the sensitivity! Like Mellencamp, the girl went to New York to transfer her dream into a reality. As with Mellencamp, New York wasn't kind to her, either. But she was trapped there; she had to remain. Mellencamp left. The dream of the Broadway stage is replaced with dancing in a sleazy bar. Her zest for life is drained. The Big Apple stamped out her dream and crushed her. Mellencamp, during his climb to the top, must have lived her frustration. Luckily, he was not defeated. Unfortunately, the Taxi Dancer was.

"I Need a Lover," the last song on the first side of *A Biography*, is a second song that appears later on the *John Cougar* album. Cougar's first big hit, this song has a chorus that many know. The speaker says he needs a lover that will not drive him nuts, who will thrill him and then leave. Her knowing when it's time to hit the road is essential if she intends to be his lover. Admitting to a level of confusion that makes his mind indifferent, he swears he won't be destroyed by the "poolroom life I'm living." To avoid defeat, the speaker lists his options as finding a job, enrolling in school, or returning back home. Then, the Cougar theme of searching for meaningful human relationships enters when he says he does not seek love or forgiveness. All he seeks is a companion to help him endure another lonely night of fearful shaking in his bedroom. When he performs this song, John Cougar Mellencamp emits a special pride, since it was his first noticeable hit. He should be proud, as the quiet strength the song conveys is an introspective, honest openness that John Mellencamp likes.

Side 2 opens with a four-minute number called "Alley of the Angels." Think about the irony within the title itself. Angels are not normally associated with alleys. An alley is normally thought of as being narrow, dark, and gloomy, hardly the habitat for angels, except John Cougar's angels. His angels on the cover of the *Uh-huh* album possess horns. So either young Mellencamp enjoys a certain element of iconoclastic image breaking or he is just ignorant about angels. My money goes with the first suspicion. Think, also, about how this alley is described by Cougar. This alley of the angels becomes a symbolic sanctuary, wherein the speaker (perhaps John is talking about himself here) can enjoy some respite from the tribulations of reality: his vulnerability, his insecurity, his fear, and his search for adult approval and human understanding. The "camp" universality of Mellencamp's lyrics seeps through this song, as do the Cougaresque empathy and hope that characterizes so much of John's writing.

Utilizing a stream-of-consciousness technique, Mellencamp writes of another sad day, of the world collapsing around him, and of being hit hard by his old man. Then the central character wonders why one has to be so tough—both physically and verbally—in order to survive. He wonders if there is a place where he could belong and be accepted for what he is, where he would not have to exist in constant fear of not measuring up to somebody else's notion of what he should be. To this end, he says that any place would prove better than where he is now, which we assume is at home.

This protagonist, fearing retribution while seeking sensitivity, questions the frequent use of physical force and abusive language to which he is apparently subjected. Instead, he yearns for self-acceptance and an escape from his feelings of inferiority. Later, Cougar follows his formula for universally tugging at the common heartstrings that unite us with humanity. Observing others, the troubled speaker puts down other kids who are such a mess, because they want to be handed the best on a silver platter, without having to learn respect or gratitude. Perhaps the allusions are trite and unoriginal, but the speaker is striving for objectivity. "Wanting the best" is taught to us as an integral part of the American way. We chase our dreams and hope for the best. Permanence and security will create happiness and contentment, at least for most of us. But we remain perpetually aware of our frailty. Says the speaker, adolescents mature, but they continue to seek that place in the sun where their physical, mental, and spiritual identity will not be shattered. In this song the alliteration of the "s" sound is effective, as it reminds us of a deflating tire. The symbol of the sun as a life-giving force is also relevant.

The fitting conclusion to the song hits us directly with the speaker's confusion. Like Everybody and Anyone, this speaker hungers for the acceptance and the approval that will make him feel important, worthwhile, and wanted. But this sensitive soul is not comfortable with the types of aggression he observes. So his refuge is in the alley of the angels. (These lyrics ring an autobiographical note also.) This metaphorical title is especially apropos because it drives the intensity of the lyrics home. The title makes us feel somewhat uncomfortable and uneasy; then, when we meet such an honest, straightforward protagonist, our uneasiness turns into shame and sorrow. The song ends on a sad note of lost hope: even the speaker's use of profanity seems to be telling us that no tunnel of light has yet appeared. The confused protagonist decides that one does not really need to be such a rough-and-tough son-of-a-bitch. On the other hand, he has not yet discovered his place in the sun. Thus the "alley of the angels" will provide temporary sanctuary for him.

A less sensitive song, running nearly five minutes, is "High C Cherrie." The young lady in the title swallows more than her share of verbal abuse from the young men in the vicinity. The boys bombard her with sexual offerings, which lead us to wonder what Cherrie has done to deserve this demeaning treatment. Has she done anything at all? Whether he or she deserves it or not, every town seems to have a symbolic scapegoat who bears the brunt of all vulgarity and directionless humor. The male speaker proudly talks, in the chorus, about his jet-black Cadillac (nice internal rhyme) that is parked out back. This guy's identity is so attached to that Cadillac that we hardly observe any personality at all, other than that which emerges as a result of owning the Cadillac. The Caddy is a source of power, intimidation, equality, and oneupmanship. This speaker uses all of these. He even offers to serve her a six-pack of Rollin' Thunder beer. Sometimes he worries that she must always remember that she was sent from heaven for the guys working at the store. Ironically, what appears to be a tender sentiment is actually, in context, a derogatory cheap shot. In my estimation, "High C Cherrie" is an overly long song, my least favorite of the entire album. But perhaps some signficant concept or symbol is eluding my attention.

Another lengthy melody, running nearly four minutes, is "Where the Sidewalk Ends." A sidewalk is a pathway, indicating direction and hope, so the destination will ultimately be reached. Asking a sexy girl to talk to him, the speaker in the song tells her, later, that he knows what he wants and she knows what he needs. If she takes him seriously, he will show her what life is like on the other side of the street. The sidewalk, and consequently the street, have symbolic value. Poetically, we could claim that a sidewalk is unending. But this sidewalk is an exception: it ends. Universally, this sidewalk could represent our lives, our hopes, our aspirations. The protagonist asks the lady how she will modify her self-concept when the sidewalk ends, since nobody will be buying anything when that happens. For this prostitute, her sidewalk will end, it seems, when her youthful beauty and her sexual sensuality are evaporated with time. A sense of emptiness and desperation permeate this ballad. Ignoring the sidewalk—the glimpse into the future—the guy acknowledges that the woman gives him strength. Maybe he sees her as a commodity to conquer, but he also recognizes that his identity is intertwined with hers. Power and confidence and self-esteem are necessary ingredients in this game we call life. Without these ingredients, our sidewalk might end too soon. The lyrics seem disjointed at times, as Mellencamp is using a stream-of-consciousness technique. In this instance, however, the technique has resulted in the song's possessing an esoteric quality that is elusive to pin down and troublesome to identify.

Such is not the case, however, with the next entry, the longest cut on the entire album. "Let Them Run Your Life" runs five seconds short of six minutes. Besides the length, though, the song is characterized by skilled piano interludes, effective symbolism, vivid imagery, and Mellencampish themes. By the time I had ever heard the *A Biography* album, I, like most Cougar fans, was already familiar with "Taxi Dancer" and "I Need a Lover." Both of those are praiseworthy numbers, to be sure. But, of the remaining eight cuts on this not-so-well–known album, "Let Them Run Your Life" is my favorite. The lyrics bring to mind more recent numbers written by John, such as "Miami," with the affluence of the girls who have such high opinions of themselves, and "Authority Song," where the central figure is constantly struggling to establish his own identity, and, indeed, any of Mellencamp's songs that promote the theme of survival, life, and/or reality. And it is typical of Cougar—shrewd though he is—that the universal collectiveness of the lyrics allows us to understand, to relate, and to question.

The adolescents are blessed with carpeted bedrooms equipped with expensive stereos and other extravagant toys. But the lyricist claims that these symbols of materialism divert his mind from reality. The reality is that he will fly through life with no real future, looking for another lonely lover to hold tightly so he can further delude himself into believing that everything is just fine. Authority figures run his life this way—substituting superficial objects as replacements for meaningful alliances. These authority figures drain the energy from their young, metaphorically cutting their throats, so as to curtail any protests and to hide the fact that they have been unsuccessful at teaching the offspring about how to deal with the ordeal of life. In a playful twist of words, Mellencamp says that uncertain worlds make it certain that adolescents (like himself) will have to kiss ass if they expect to survive. No free rides exist; tough exteriors are essential. The final stanza introduces two typical adolescents—Jay Dee and Ruda Juda—who struggle with the task of challenging their inner moxie. The last line of the song, asking if one must fight for the rest of his life, captures the utter disillusionment of a teenager's view of society, as well as his view of reality.

Stylistically, "Let Them Run Your Life" is a series of shifting moods. In the opening scene, with the carpeted bedroom and the stereos (symbols of middle-class success), the mood is controlled, yet angry. The speaker stresses the youth of the two adolescents by saying "girls and boys" rather than the more colloquial "boys and girls." But look at the function of these hundred-dollar toys: the adult figures shower kids with these extravagant but meaningless gifts so as to muddy the waters by taking the kids' thoughts away from the future. The toys provide them with a socially acceptable avenue of pure escapism. Reality, offering shaky futures at best, forces them to crawl into cocoons of protectionism. The speaker regrets this ironic observation, but confesses that it is true. The mood has shifted to one of fear. This game of life is seen as a street race, where we look for a lonely lover to embrace for the night. The alliteration of the "l" assists the sound imagery, as do the rhyming words. This lover, not permanent, is like the expensive toys: the lover deludes us into believing that all is well, when, in reality, we are so distantly removed from reality that the speaker says we are about to lose our minds. This is frightening. Our regulated minds—what a choice image of symbolic depth—are indeed controlled by the items (the toys and the lovers) that we utilize to carry out our escape. Over the long haul, however, these fragile and contrived artifacts of escapism prove to be failures. Eventually, we must come to grips with the sobering fact that this behavior will carry us to no meaningful conclusion.

The chorus uses the indefinite pronoun *them*. Who is "them"? Does *them* refer to our parents? After all, they provide the carpeting, the stereos, and the toys. Or does *them* refer to the symbols of materialism themselves? Actually, we can have it either way. *Them* could even imply a reference to any authority figure—teachers, ministers, businessmen, police, or whomever. This elusive, vague, indefinable *them*, found in both the title and the chorus, continues the vivid imagery, as we witness a symbolic slashing of our throats. An upsetting but most appropriate metaphor, the sharp and piercing "parental carving knife" turns our basic instinctual fears into a bizarre feeling of extreme edginess. A "parental carving knife" is stressfully disturbing, particularly since we, the youth, are the ones being carved in a genocidal death. Mellencamp does not mean to suggest a literal death here, but he does imply a symbolic death that comes about because we are blinded by the superficial manifestations of materialism, which isolate us from the harsh realities that are ready and waiting to gobble us up and spit us out. Cougar's chorus, as well as the rest of the lyrics, are superb examples of his naturalistic tendencies in his songs. Naturalism, like John himself, is a byproduct of a society that really wants us to succeed on our own. Today naturalism remains a potent force in both our literature and in our thinking. And naturalism makes John's chorus a beautiful piece of poetry, as well as a functional thematic springboard.

The second stanza is noteworthy for three reasons. First, John cleverly uses internal rhyme to please our ears and force us to take notice. For example, John includes phrases such as "to deal with the ordeal" and "in this world of uncertainties you can be certain." A technique like this would become monotonous if used too frequently, but Cougar is shrewd enough not to overplay his hand. The immediate repetition of the words *deal* and *certain* adds emphasis to the lyrics. Second, John also utilizes repetition as an effective technique. The unnamed *they* begins many of the lines in the stanza. This repetition creates drama. The pronoun *you* also saturates this stanza. Again, though, this repetition is acceptable because it is only in this stanza and because Cougar possesses a sixth sense that allows him to know when enough is enough. As an object of a preposition, as an indirect object, as a subject, or in whatever capacity, the lyrics keep driving the concept of "you" directly home. This "you," as we know, can be Anybody, another aspect of John's songwriting skill and popular appeal. Third, Mellencamp's theme of survival appears in this underrated song. To survive, one must humble himself before the authorities (colloquially presented by John with the kissing-ass image) and be a "real man," possessing strength and confidence and convictions.

After a second rendition of the chorus, the third and final verse begins. This stanza is sung at a faster, more aggressive tempo, reflecting the dramatic climax of the song and the heightened anger of the speaker. The unidentified "you" in the previous stanzas now becomes specific individuals. Jay Dee, for example, is locked in his soul, a metaphorical hotel of no exits. Nice metaphor, John! Ruda Juda attempts an escape with alcohol, but lies unconscious on the floor. The speaker asks for somebody to remove her alcohol (described metaphorically as a gun, a suicidal death wish for escape) and take her home. But Jay Dee and Ruda Juda are symbolic representations of us. Could those names be those of real people, anyway? John's sixth sense tells him to move away from so much *you*, so he selects two names, a male and a female, to symbolically represent Everybody in his theme of universality and common identity.

The rapid tempo of this stanza is clever, not only for variety, but also to deliver the theme. The song ends with the speaker—dare I suggest that John is writing about himself—confessing the fact that he is so misunderstood by others (parents and friends) that he is pleased to still be alive. Again, John's prolife theme is apparent. But the initiation of this young protagonist (John, in my estimation) is so decisive and so earned that we are proud of the individual and pray that he now earns the understanding he has been seeking. The last musical bars begin to fade when we hear John voice the proverbial question about the balance between romanticism and realism. Will the rest of his life be typified by fighting? Ultimately, and optimistically, listeners realize that this confused symbolic Everybody will triumph.

The last cut on the album, "Good Night," is also the shortest. The two-minute length of this song is particularly noticeable on an album where the ten numbers average four minutes in length. The easygoing tempo serves to focus our attention onto the wet, chilly night as the speaker bids adieu to his companion. Using the poetic device of personification, Cougar has the protagonist begin by slowly lamenting the truth: as the cab picks him up on a rainy night, he observes the darkness being devoured by the approaching daylight. Daybreak is at hand, so we assume the couple have spent the night together. City workers are beginning to clean the streets. The protagonist observes an elderly vagrant who lies asleep on the street corner, having spent the dreary, rainy night wrapped in rags and newspaper. What a contrast betweeen this homeless wretch and the observant narrator.

Then, as night gives way to daylight more and more, the narrator bids his lover goodnight as the morning light brings mobs of people out onto the streets. These people rob the lovers of their privacy, coaxing the narrator to mutter to himself.

This ending, with its obscene utterance, was a surprise to me when I heard the song for the first time. Yet the more I contemplate the contrast in events (night to day and empty streets to buzzing city), the more I appreciate the symbolic significance of the final line. The "crowd of people" represents our impersonal society. As morning begins, these hordes begin to fill the streets. But the speaker regrets this change, as he prefers the streets to be dark and empty. Hence the "oh, shit" expresses his chagrin. The title, we now realize, has a double meaning. On a blanket, superficial, literal level, the title means he is merely telling his girl "goodnight." But on a deeper, more symbolic level, the night itself is good; normally night and darkness are indicative of evil, as murderers, rapists, and werewolves come out at night. But the speaker in this verse enjoys the privacy and the solace that the night provides. Hence night is good. This double meaning to the title comes as a surprise also since the glorification of the night is not made totally apparent until this last line of the song. All in all, "Good Night" is a fine song. It is not great, perhaps, and it would not lend itself to a popular video format, but the song does possess vivid, everyday images, and it does convey sincere, human sentiments.

Because *Chestnut Street Incident* did not sell well, a decision was made to release *A Biography* only in England and in other selected parts of Europe. This explains why copies of *A Biography* are so difficult to locate today. The album cover pictures a moody "Johnny Cougar" standing in full view of the camera, against a brown backdrop. His haunting, sexy eyes look at us directly, yet we do not feel intimidated or fearful. We feel comfortable and friendly. With *Chestnut Street Incident* and *The Kid Inside* readily available in American record bins, perhaps there is some reason to hope that *A Biography* will become available. Whether it does or not, the album is worth owning, not because it is so great of itself, but because it is part of the progressive evolution of John Cougar Mellencamp as a writer, a singer, and a performer. The ten songs run over forty minutes, which is unusual in and of itself. But the real forte of *A Biography* is the insight it provides into the themes and poetic techniques that we so readily associate with John Cougar Mellencamp.

CHAPTER TEN

John Cougar
Riva, 1979

The problem with the album carrying the John Cougar name as its title is not so much that the 1979 release is underrated. The problem is that his first album released in the United States, through Riva, is so regretfully ignored and overlooked. Bargain-bin shoppers should keep their eyes pealed for this one. The cover shows a facial closeup of an unshaven Cougar with what is presumably his trademark Marlboro dangling from his mouth. The back cover shows a shot from the waist up, with Cougar's right hand atop his long hair, a pose somewhat reminiscent of his idol, James Dean. The inside jacket, which contains the words to the ten numbers, all written by John himself, includes other shots of John performing. He emits energy and enthusiasm, embracing music, a love of his life.

"A Little Night Dancin'" opens the album. A concise song with biblical allusions to Zion and Sodom and Gomorrah, plus a fantasy allusion to Cinderella, the narrative unfolds with a story of cocaine-induced euphoria. The drummer keeps the beat for the night dancing that manages to keep the cast attuned somewhat to reality. Unfortunately, the independence and the freedom here are not real, since they are the result of an escapist's use of drugs.

Also not real is the love encounter of the next song, "Small

Paradise." The selection of the word *small* is useful, as the word alters its meaning in the song. The personification of the neon sign that blinks in the pouring rain is dramatically used to color a setting for the speaker to meet a prostitute, with whom we presume he will spend the night. As he yearns for something more than physical sexual encounters, he says that what they have together is not love, but it isn't too bad. The coolness of the night, the wildness of the whiskey, and the dampness of the rain culminate in a cold, harsh, uncomfortable environment. This is a naturalism of sorts—one that hungers for a romantic reality.

The lyrics of the third number, "Miami," are well known to some fans. Miami has girls toasting their skin in the sun as they wait for more money from their fathers back home. Maintaining appearances is of tantamount importance. These attractive females are gorgeous to look at, but impossible to hold closely. Their conceit, however, dissipates at night, as they search for companionship in bars. Their fun-loving style and their high-fashion clothes do not bless them with the real sparks that life requires. They seek love, understanding, and appreciation, not sex, alienation, and one-night stands. Ironically, they are not real, either, as they peel away their armor (clothes) inside their bedrooms, yet cannot be seen in public associating with such people as the rejected narrator/protagonist.

Thoughts of Miami bring thoughts of sandy beaches and resort hotels to mind. The first stanza depicts an undercurrent of defiance and hatred directed toward these "rich" brats whose dads shell out money for them to appear lavish. "Toasting their flesh in the sun" is one fine metaphor also. These girls are beautiful yet conceited, he observes. But then why are they alone in a bar, dreaming about companionship? Cougar's initial dislike for them melts into empathy when he sees they, too, are really coping with loneliness and alienation. Wearing beautiful clothes and boasting impressive dreams, they turn to somebody like him once they are safely hidden in the crowd. Mellencamp has a tough time accepting these pseudoairs. Many of us do. But Mellencamp also sees beneath the fakery and the emptiness and the fantasy. Social class doesn't insulate one from having to endure the hurts and the pains these folks feel.

The best entry on side 1 is the fourth cut, "The Great Midwest." On one hand, the lyrics attack the values held by the people living in the midwest: unions, church, cookouts, materialism. On the other hand, the lyrics accept and respect the wishes of the individual who finds contentment with that routine, while at the same time honoring the courage of the individual (someone like Mellencamp) who makes a conscious decision to seek something better. In my opinion, "The Great Midwest" is a moving ballad, a social statement, and a fair appraisal of reality.

According to the chorus of Mellencamp's song, the Great Midwest, cornfields and all, is either five years ahead of the times or twenty-five years behind. Mellencamp claims to be uncertain himself, even though he sees the life-style as being somewhat slower than those of the rest of the country. Union cards must guarantee a certain security, thus allowing the less-frenzied pace. After church, at Sunday-afternoon barbecues, the young men brag about their powerful cars, their hefty paychecks, their mistreatment of their girl friends, and their cycle of partying, drinking, and fighting. Mellencamp offers a sour twist, indeed, as he concludes that the Great Midwest, with all its security and comforts, is plagued by an inner upheaval that prevents citizens from knowing themselves. Individuals sacrifice their physical selves, as well as their spiritual souls, in order to live the so-called life-style of the successful. Although the lyrics are permeated by a sense of remorse and regret, Mellencamp says he is not complaining or bragging. He is merely stating factual details. On the other hand, he thinks he wants to escape, to avoid sticking around and depending upon friends in important positions to offer him some upward mobility. He is willing to work, and he realizes he may be running away from himself, but he needs to know if he will be a success or a failure once he abandons the protective womb offered by the unions. At this stage in his life, he is unwilling to merely "get by" (survive); he is also unwilling to trade his happiness for the security and the money that his life-style promises. The independent streak wins out; he leaves, to venture out on his own.

Interesting, isn't it, how differently people see the role of big business? Yes, we now question the cost—human, not just financial—of big business. We didn't use to do this; now, however, we do. Does a corporation—say, General Motors, for example—coerce its workers, the United Auto Workers, to sacrifice personal contentment for high wages? Is the Midwestern lifestyle, one of materialism and routines, also one that robs us of our body and soul?

The first three lines of the bridge shed light on young Mellencamp's viewpoint. He is neither complaining nor blaming, but hopes to be understood. He merely accepts life as it is here, while being frightened of his role in it. So, as young John left the farmlands of Seymour, the speaker in the song leaves the homeland also. Many midwesterners tend to lead comfortable lives, but, yes, they pay a price in terms of the environmental damage and air pollution. And many adults who have worked for these corporations harbor dreams of something better for their own children. John Cougar is uncannily fair in this song, as he appears to understand and relate to both sides of the dilemma. This objectiveness, however, conceals his true feelings about the relationship of individuals to their jobs.

After listening to the closing song on side 1, called, "Do You Think That's Fair?" our obvious question is, "Fair for whom?" as we know that life is not always predicated on our own self-serving ideas of what is just and fair. Once all is said and done, Cougar himself seems to empathize with the female protagonist, yet he realizes that she deserves what she ends up with. A sexual poetic justice, one assumes.

The narrative is about a married lady who also has a boyfriend. The speaker has twenty-five dollars he is willing to spend on her, but knows that she cheats on all her lovers. He has been there, also, however, so he claims to understand. Yet, in the chorus, he asks if she thinks all of this is fair. Do they have to be so lonely and so scared, he wonders. Can they make this situation turn out like they want? Are they even in touch with what they want? Not being sure, they each go their separate ways. Cougar poignantly expresses his anxiety when he wonders about the way Time always destroys Infatuation. Metaphorically, her life becomes a masquerade, hiding the real her from everybody. He offers friendly advice to her—as old age approaches, not to expect too much from any of these new lovers. The masquerade will result in nobody caring.

But is this fair? Fair for the husband? The woman? The speaker in the poem? The other lovers? For anyone? The speaker has grown up, seen the light, and acted accordingly. The woman is an object of sympathy, to be sure, an insecure woman who has allowed her self-doubts and indecision to destroy whatever happiness she might have once found. Is this fair? Is life fair? This is life, fair or not. These traumatic crises occur, ruining desperate lives in the process. This is a heavy song by Cougar, which deals with life and its naturalistic realities.

"I Need a Lover" opens side 2—the better of the two sides, in my estimation. Pat Benatar scored a hit with this song. Today John pridefully acknowledges that Benatar's hit generated enough royalties for him to buy a house for himself and his family. This early taste of success fills the soul with a drive to nurture one's creative genius. Like other songs from the pen of Mellencamp, "I Need a Lover" is characterized by certain "camp" themes: survival, endurance, loneliness, the search for recognition and understanding, as well as the thrill and pleasure of fornication. The protagonist admits that his mind is indifferent as he wanders through the "human jungle" of the city streets at night. Once again, Mellencamp has plucked the strings of our collective psyche and struck financial paydirt.

"Welcome to Chinatown" also appeals to me. The speaker seems to personify a contradiction of innocence and guilt. Yet the speaker is telling us about his sexual lust, which is indulged in on a trip to a Chinese brothel with a group of his buddies. Many males can relate to this narrative—either through direct experience or through indirect fantasy. On a cool evening, the protagonist attends a party with several buddies. They end up at a Chinese brothel, where the buddies warn him about the habits of the Chinese: drugs and drink. So he should keep cool, they alert him. The protagonist, an antihero typical of Mellencamp's speakers, is enthusiastic about the venture. He even admits that he is not particularly selective when chosing sexual partners. He'll flip-flop with anybody, as long as no strings are attached. The slit-eyed woman at the brothel was old and smart, but she showed him a good time. He likens the encounter to a shaking rickshaw ride. She pushed her fingers down his throat, whispered into his ear, and made him think he had died and entered heaven. The sexual ecstasy was dynamite; he must have imagined the earth to be moving. She kept telling him he was welcome in Chinatown, that she was going to lay his body down. She delivered on all her promises! He felt sexually awakened.

A young man's lust initiates his reentry (no pun intended) into sexual pursuits. The boy and his friends reveal their lack of knowledge with their stereotyped concept of the Chinese. But the encounter was pleasant: "like some rickshaw ride" is an appropriate yet humorous simile. The ecstasy made him think he had died and gone to heaven. Perhaps the song is repulsive to some, but it deals directly and honestly with real people, real situations, and, whether we admit it or not, real solutions. John Cougar Mellencamp folds a plethora of emotions into this song: passion, comradery, prejudice, amorality, ecstasy, and satisfaction. I think John intended the song to be fun and heartening, rather than offensive and desperate.

Unlike "Welcome to Chinatown," "Sugar Marie" is perhaps Cougar's greatest tribute to a woman. After the protagonist is off his loser's job, he goes with a buddy named Jeffrey Jack to the local dance hall. Drinking tequila sunrises, he'll eventually meet Sugar Marie, the tremendous lady who is so fantastic that she makes him forget about himself and his own needs. He loves her and cares for her and feels right when in her presence. She understands him, accepts him, and does not question him. Perhaps the search for love and commitment has ended! Sugar Marie works at the truck stop, hustling Cokes and hamburgers, but her heart belongs to the lucky guy in the song. The bridge of the song expresses this love in no uncertain terms: Sugar

Marie has earned this guy's admiration and respect because she has taught him how to respect himself. She has proven to him that he is not an island unto himself, that he does need somebody. One wonders if Sugar Marie is totally imaginary or if she is/was a part of John Cougar Mellencamp's life.

"Sugar Marie" is a fitting tribute to a compatible couple. She makes him like himself and forget about himself. Any girl, as these songs show, can serve as a sex kitten; but finding a devoted woman who will love and accept him without reservation and without judgment is a personal triumph for him. "Sugar Marie," like "Welcome to Chinatown," is intended to be a happy song, making us feel hopeful about life and confident in ourselves. To me, skill is needed to write two songs with such similar impact, yet with such dissimilar moods. Nice going, John!

"Pray For Me" will have different meanings for different people. God reprimands Moses for the behavior of man. Shakespeare decides to become a bricklayer or a groupie. Cain and Abel play croquet. Everything seems incongruous. Images are changing. Pleasure seekers rule. But the speaker—Mellencamp himself, perhaps—asks for prayers. With nothing to count on, with nothing being permanent, the protagonist seeks rationality, security, and tenderness. His fear is best expressed in the chorus, where he welcomes any prayers that anybody might wish to offer on his behalf.

The vulnerability of living proves terrifying to the speaker. Nothing is sacred, even a representative of the church. Prostitution invades society. But where is tenderness? Where is life? One of Cougar's enviable talents is his ability to assail us with contradictions: here—if one interprets the song on the assumption that Cougar is using the speaker to convey his own thoughts and fears and hopes—he is both tough and tame, streetwise and innocent. This ability helps to define Cougar's appeal. To understand him is to appreciate him.

The last of the ten songs on the *John Cougar* album, my favorite, is titled "Taxi Dancer." Because this ballad appeared on the earlier album called *A Biography*, little needs to be said here. John Mellencamp, like myself, likes "Taxi Dancer," but he becomes frustrated when some audiences reject the song. In Glasgow, Scotland, for example, fans boo and throw things when John sings "Taxi Dancer." Glasgow is in industrial area, where many fans want rock and roll, not ballads. Mellencamp must, therefore, be cautious about the nature of his audience prior to adding "Taxi Dancer" to the agenda.

The runtlike rocker from the Hoosier state scored with the *John Cougar* album, albeit not as measured by the traditional barometer of financial returns. The album failed to sell in large numbers. However, the album did introduce John Mellencamp, alias John Cougar, to the American public. And, naturally, when the album introduced John, it also introduced his lyrics, his band, his style, and his flamboyance. This generated some controversy, largely through misunderstanding, but John has weathered the criticism and proven his versatility and his talent. John's music is a populist form of rock unencumbered by pretention and distraction. John's band, The Zone, is a compatible group whose members seem to enjoy performing. John's style is informal, yet aggressive; sensitive, yet vivid; angry, yet not hateful. John's boozy-edged, growling voice is both mysterious and sexy. All of these qualities gush forth on the *John Cougar* album, but they gush in a palatable manner. Instead of overwhelming us, these qualities show us that John Mellencamp, even under a different name, smells as sweet. Like any true artist, like any true performer, John Cougar Mellencamp, even with his identity complex, commands the performance under his control, yet does not dominate the show. This is rock at its finest!

CHAPTER ELEVEN

Nothing Matters and What if It Did?
Riva, 1980

Steve Cropper is the producer of this release. The album only sold a half-million copies or so, but like the previous releases, particularly *John Cougar*, the album placed John's name before the public. Few artists score big the first time a record is released; those who do tend to score big, then fade away. True, there are exceptions to this generality, as there are to any generality. But there is an element of truth to the concept that those stars who endure in the field usually struggled to the top. John Cougar impresses me as being this kind of star. *Nothing Matters and What if It Did?* consists of nine songs, one of which was not written by John. The opening song, "Hot Night in a Cold Town," was written by Geoffrey Cushing-Murray.

One of the hits from the *Nothing Matters* album is called "Ain't Even Done with the Night." Again, people relate to this song. A young boy is afraid that his first sexual "performance" will not satisfy the girl, whom he sees as more experienced. Not only can we relate to his trepidation and inadequacy, but we can also laugh at our own adolescent past. Cougar has tossed a highly successful commercial formula at us here, yet the listener sympathizes with the boy and with the girl. Cougar's opening simile is simple; the vocalulary is simple; the song is so humanly simple that we enjoy it.

The lyrics of "Ain't Even Done with the Night" focus upon the young man's pleasure. Hearts beating loudly and the radio playing, the girl encourages the boy to make her happy. Inexperienced, he is uncertain as to whether or not he is performing adequately—whether or not he is satisfying her sexual drive. Since he is aware of no fancy tricks or one-liner come-ons, he must depend upon his own conditioned responses.

Simple lyrics. Simple poetic devices, like internal rhyme and repetition. Simple people. Simple problem. Cougar's favorite word must be *well*, a word he uses frequently in other songs also. The extra syllable must help keep the rhythm and the beat. Simplicity aside, the humanness and the universality cannot be overlooked. Maybe the girl in this song should team up with "Jack and Diane." Or Diane team up with the boy? Talk about a hot night!

"Don't Misunderstand Me" sounds possibly autobiographical again. John's personal life was in somewhat of an upheaval at the time this song was written, around 1980 or 1981. The song portrays two people who love and admire each other failing miserably at continuing on together. Some time after the release of the album, John confessed that he was unhappy with the finished product. Explaining his dissatisfaction, he remarks:

> Nothing sounded the same from track to track. The drums didn't sound the same; the guitars didn't sound the same. Rather than fight with somebody at this point in my life—I was getting divorced, I was getting married, a thousand things were going on—I figured next time out, I'd do it myself. I knew enough about the business by then, enough about how my records should sound, to just do it.[1]

Some critics see this as John's strong confidence. Nevertheless, the stage was set for the appearance of *American Fool*, his blockbuster.

But isn't it possible that "Don't Misunderstand Me" is a love song to John's first wife, Priscilla? Nobody knows for certain, of course, save John himself. But the couple in this song are splitting, despite their affections for each other. The guy confesses to her that he lacks maturity, tells lies, breaks promises, and behaves irresponsibly. Pleading, he wants to know what he can say to convince her to stay. Even the listener wonders why she would even think about staying, since feeling sorry for him is certainly not a valid reason for sacrificing her own happiness.

The chorus just pleads for her not to misunderstand him. Then the speaker talks again, saying to her that she says she loves him, but can't go on living the way they are. Remember, for a while, John lived on unemployment checks, with no personal drive at all. They lived at the home of the in-laws, with John throwing Frisbees and playing in his band. From the viewpoint of the father-in-law, how long would you tolerate this lackadaisical slovenliness? In the last stanza, the male speaker asks the girl to tolerate his childishness, because he is going to triumph, to prove victorious, to escape from this messy, unpleasant reality. John, luckily, did succeed at his dream. But, if you were the girl, would you stick it out with him?

The other hit on the album is titled "This Time." The innocent girl meets the experienced boy, and surprise, surprise, the boy loses! It takes courage for the speaker to imply that he regrets the loss of her fresh innocence.

The highly repetitious chorus exhorts this guy's friends to really believe that "this time," he really is in love. But nobody really believes the braggart Romeo. At the end, in fact, we generally feel that she was lucky not to fall for his lies. She is too good for him; he begins to realize this and, in the last two lines, pays tribute to the beautiful quality that he has lost. Toward the end, he says she was too intelligent to believe all his lies, while he was too drunk to realize what was happening. He only hopes that she never loses her innocence and sense of humor.

The self-indulgent, noncommittal braggart has begun to fall in love with her. But before he attuned himself to his own emotions, he had lost her. Realizing his faults, he praises, in her, the beautiful, innocent laughter that he wishes was within him. On one hand, we feel glad for the girl and sad for the boy. After all, they may have been great together. On the other hand, the insincerity and the lightheartedness of the boy are unlikely to make him appealing to a person like her. Thus he deserved to loose her. Poetic justice.

The final cut on side 1 portrays a weak, insecure man trying to convince his girl friend not to leave him. The role reversal here, with the man being subordinate to the woman, is intriguing. John possesses an uncanny insight into a female's psyche. The speaker in "Make Me Feel" admits that they have wasted too much of their time together. Then he begs her to thrill him as he likes to be thrilled, to make him feel the way he felt when their relationship began.

The standard a-b-a-b rhyme scheme of the quatrains is not particularly unusual, but there seems to be little if any recognition, on the speaker's part, of his responsibility to control and guide his feelings. Thus the speaker continues with his plea. He wonders why he is losing her. Is there some other man? Has she changed her plans? Have her dreams and goals outgrown his limited viewpoint?

This possessiveness of his is both unappealing and unadmirable. As in "This Time," we seem to side with the honest, strong-willed female. All this guy seems to care about is his own feelings. The song concludes, with no regrets from us, with a final cry. He begs her to stay, to hear him out, to stay that night and hold him in her hands.

With the intensity of his insecurity, wouldn't you think he would want her to hold him in her arms? The only explanation for Mellencamp's use of the word *hands* that I can glean is for masturbatory purposes. In this case, *me* would refer to his penis and the word *feel* in the title and throughout the song would take on a totally new dimension. But the word *hands* has always struck me by surprise.

Of course, if masturbation is his goal, then the meaning of the song is altered. Instead of a longer relationship coming to an end, because of another man in her life or whatever, he is merely trying to lay a guilt trip on her for not wanting to make him "feel" the way he wants to feel. Also, with this interpretation of their sexual encounter, the line "Make me feel like I did in the start" could refer to the initial masturbatory experiences that a boy has. Most boys masturbate before they experience intercourse. With either interpretation of the song, however, the girl comes out on top (no pun intended) as the winner of the relationship. His possessiveness and his self-centeredness are too much to expect any girl to accept. She flees from these entrapments, not from his sexual desires. But fleeing was bright, on her part!

The flip side opens with "To M.G. (Wherever She May Be)." Oldtimers are reminded of Jimmy Durante's "Goodnight, Mrs. Calabash, wherever you are." The speaker here is male, but he is admirable. His sensitivity is a strength, his understanding a plus. M.G., I was told, is Margaret Goen, a former girlfriend of John's who is now married. She must be a remarkable lady.

Watching television, the speaker sees a beautiful actress who reminded him of this girl whom he addresses in the song. This lost lover has since married another man, one who is apparently successful and affluent. She, too, possessed an innocent laughter that he hopes will be nurtured as she grows older; regretfully, he realizes that so much time has floated by that he might not even recognize her any longer. But the fond memories of their days in junior high have remained with him. Their evenings underneath the front porch may not have been a passionate love affair, but at the time, they seemed like they were. As he is older and wiser now, his perspective is more rational; he only hopes that she makes her husband feel as warm as her sweet kisses made him feel back when he was fifteen and younger.

My evaluation places "To M.G." far above "This Time" in the hit category, but "To M.G." fizzled. Two qualities appeal. First, the narrative of the ballad, with its details being shown in a movielike flashback, is impressive and effective. Second, the narrator/protagonist is a bundle of contradictions, yet still likable and memorable. He has an enviable sexiness, yet he is coy. He has an innocence, yet he is wise. He is quiet, yet he controls. These are fine qualities in a superb mixture. After all these years, he admires her smile, her actions, and her desires. No apparent connection exists between this song and "This Time," but

Cougar uses the "innocent laughter" allusion in both. Time is a powerful force, a tremendous teacher. Now, the man/boy knows that the relationship was not really that big a deal, but what boy doesn't remember the first kiss he received from a girl? What boy didn't make more out of that first kiss than was really there? But he truly admires and loves her and hopes that she makes her husband feel as warm and as important as she made him feel. What a laudable compliment to this extraordinary lady.

Songs like "To M.G. (Wherever She May Be)" show John Cougar Mellencamp at his best. The sex may be extramarital, but it is not void of feeling. And the people involved, at least the protagonist, learn something worth knowing about the frailty of life and the importance of dreams. They also grow in self-awareness and self-esteem, which makes them better and happier human beings.

Much energy bursts forth in "Tonight." The speaker rises, determined not to be too late for work because the boss is such a mean SOB. At five, he'll see his girl again. She is so beautiful that she has to be a sin, he thinks. Later that evening, at the East Street Montgomery Pier, she pulls him close and whispers into his ear for him to move closer, so she can shove her "pussy" right into his face. Her sexuality has been aroused, so he is the boy she hopes will make her feel alive. This is a nice compliment for her to pay to him, but the song seems superficial and meaningless. True, we all have bad days at work and we all enjoy the end of the workday. But "Tonight" lacks depth and revelation, even though it deals with a common occurrence.

A sad but hopeful song is "Wild Angel." The two words don't seem congruous: Is she wild? Is she an angel? How can she be both? But she needs closeness and she needs tenderness. Edgar Allan Poe would say the single, dominate effect is sympathy. These wild angels cruise around in beat-up automobiles, throwing kisses, but the telltale signs of age [wrinkles] are beginning to become apparent. Because of this reality, the speaker wants one particular angel to reach out to him.

This opening stanza conveys intense empathy and understanding from the speaker. Another admirable quality about

"Wild Angel" is that Cougar does not use the word *well* even once! Time is running out for this woman to contact her own feelings, to define what she desires out of life. The opening line of the second stanza is unusual and mysterious. She runs through the darkness, hoping her weakness will disappear by morning. This undefined weakness, her Waterloo, creates mystery. Toward the end, the speaker pleads with her again, as time runs out. He begs the girl to reach out to him before time runs out. He cares for her, but the days are zooming by so rapidly. This lady is so fortunate to have such a caring, patient friend. Our sympathy yearns for her to accept his kindness and allow him to help. If she refuses his offer, we fear she will never progress to first base.

The most controversial cut on the album happens to be the last cut. Called "Cheap Shot," the song directly criticizes the record companies. It is a bitter attack, and one is not surprised to learn that Phonogram was not overjoyed with the idea of manufacturing and marketing the song. Apparently, John did make one concession: he dropped "The Record Company Song" as a subtitle to the song. But in the song, John mouths some lines that do not appear on the jacket's printed lyrics. First, on the record jacket, we are informed about the record company going out of business because the records are overpriced. The band members need daytime jobs in order to survive. Disk jockeys don't give their record air time because they are not crazy about the product either. But high prices are not the only reason for the bankruptcy of the record company. Because the company devoted too much attention to popular trends, ignoring progressive innovations, the business in general suffers. *Rolling Stone* has gathered moss: it has a glossy look now.

Can a bitter song like this be taken too seriously? Are records priced too high? If they are, whose fault is it? Are the program directors overly worried about going by the book? Is there no more progressive music? If not, is the record business to blame for the loss? Phonogram showed wisdom to release the cut. True, it is hostile and aggressive, but who would take the lyrics seriously? They are overly bitter, lacking credibility. Mellencamp's frustration with the name change to Cougar is, to some extent, understandable. But name changes are certainly not unheard of in the entertainment business, plus *Cougar* has a sexy, short, aggressive animalism in it. *Mellencamp* is longer, less memorable, and, consequently, less commercial. Only speculation can render a guess as to whether John Cougar Mellencamp would be where he is today if Tony DeFries never entered the picture. Thus, John's song, albeit hostile and bitter, was an emotional pressure release to vent some inner rage. John's rage will subside. He'll probably never be overly chummy with the record company personnel, but even that conflict will meld toward a middle ground of compromise and understanding.

Nothing Matters and What if It Did? is by no means a great album, but it apparently forced John himself into making some tough decisions about his less-than-phenomenal career and about coming to terms with his own personal self-esteem and ability to control his own professional destiny. Inexperienced in the business he was, but unknowing about what he wanted he was not. The challenge to put up or shut up was brewing to a head. The stage was set. John's cards were all going to be faceup on the table. The story begins an upturn here, as the next album, *American Fool*, hit.

CHAPTER TWELVE

American Fool
Riva, 1982

Wow! Did *American Fool* ever hit! The album, released in 1982, was produced by John Cougar Mellencamp and Don Gehman. Note the use of "Mellencamp." John's given name does *not* appear on the front cover, but it does appear in reasonably big print, highly noticeable, in the lower middle of the back side. The album was manufactured and marketed by Poly Gram. Poly Gram was wise to possess the courage to allow John the license and freedom to prove his talents. A star producing his own albums is not nearly as uncommon as it used to be, but John is the type of competitive spirit who thrives on this type of responsibility and risk.

Besides introducing his real name to his fans, the *American Fool* album enjoyed other triumphs. First, John won two Grammy Awards: one for "Hurts So Good" and one for "Jack and Diane." Second, this smashing and long-awaited success proved to John and to the members of The Zone that their musical ability, combined chemistry, and general appeal were a viable commodity in the commercial marketplace of music videos and rock hits. Third, whatever financial worries the guys may have been having at the time could be pretty much forgotten about. Fourth, this success is the type of force that would enhance John's creative push, guaranteeing that we would see even better albums spewing from the pen of John Cougar Mellencamp. Fifth, the greenhorn from Seymour became a proven influence on the contemporary rock scene. This, in itself, is a great triumph!

"Hurts So Good" is a fantastic, somewhat sophomoric song that is easy to sing along with. This is part of its appeal. Rock fans even enjoyed the contradictory paradox of the title. The greenhorn was on a roll! Today almost any rock fan knows the opening two lines and the chorus of this melody. This is a charming Mellencamp, as opposed to a bitter Mellencamp.

The opening lines of "Hurts So Good" inform us that the speaker acted like a child when he was a kid and now, as an older person, he yearns for those youthful days. Remembering the girl he had then, he recalls all the enjoyable pastimes that made him "hurt so good." Love isn't always what you expect, he tells her as he asks her to sink her teeth into his bones. He has no big plans in mind other than the immediate gratification they can offer each other.

For my money, Mellencamp being simplistic and sophomoric is not all bad news. Granted, the song possesses no profound greatness, but the fun-loving boy seems to be betting his all on convincing the girl that oral sex is worth trying. The second line of the chorus, plus the paradoxical nature of the title, provide justification for this conclusion. And then the young girl is apparently not without experience. So is she open to some experimentation?

The second smash hit on the *American Fool* album is "Jack and Diane." Cougar toys with our emotions, since he convinces us, through the lyrics, to like Jack and Diane. Cougar also provides us with two adolescents who are so much like ourselves that we identify with the song. Cougar opens the hit with his mellow voice, introducing the couple: Jack and Diane, the subjects of this song, are two teenagers from the Midwest. Jack plans on being a football star; Diane is a debutante. Both are boy-and-girl-next-door types. How can we not like these two? Is the Heartland his hometown of Seymour? Does it matter, one way or the other? After a chili dog at the Tastee Freeze, Jackie suggests that he and Diane mess around behind the shade trees. Her "Bobby Brooks" are supposed to be removed ("dribble off"), allowing him to do whatever he pleases. The choice of the word *dribble* is a stroke of genius. After the trip to the privacy behind the trees, Jackie organizes his thoughts then rubs his hand through his hair, imitating Mellencamp's hero, James Dean. Like John himself, Jackie admires and sometimes imitates James Dean, the young actor who died a tragic death in a car accident in 1955.

Probably the most memorable and catchy and oft-quoted lines from "Jack and Diane" are the chorus itself and the bridge. The chorus is the famous one-liner that John discussed on "Good Morning America." Seldom does one line create such an impact. Toward the end of the memorable song is a bridge that is highly effective, symbolically and literally, in both the song itself and the popular video. Mellencamp praises rock and roll, asking the Bible Belt to offer salvation to his soul. Since reality forces us into adulthood so soon, Mellencamp advises adolescents to hang onto their youth as long as possible.

After this bridge, the chorus is repeated twice, then Cougar reminds us, sorrowfully, that Jack and Diane were trying to survive the best they knew how. Even though the relationship between Jack and Diane fell to ruin—or, shall we say, came crumblin' down—we respect Jack and Diane for doing their best and sympathize with them because their best was not enough. The third line of the bridge houses the disputed reference to "sixteen." On "Good Morning America," John claimed that he meant that we should hang on to *any* age we enjoyed. But this statement detracts from the song. "Jack and Diane" applauds the merriment and fun, the anticipation and the participation, the innocence and simplicity of age sixteen. John might well believe that we should hang onto any age we liked best. But this is not what he is actually saying in "Jack and Diane."

Although "Hurts So Good" and "Jack and Diane" were bigger blockbusters than "Hand to Hold on To," even this song helped *American Fool* go platinum. The opening verse reminds us to accept life easily and always be cool, even if we are merely pretending. Much of the remainder of the song is a fun, nonsensical series of vivid, brief images. Pick up in the middle of the number, with a series of fantasy-fun dreams: being financially solvent, betting on the horse races, becoming president of the United Nations, working in Hollywood, driving a four-wheel into the mud. With all this escapism, however, one still needs a "hand to hold on to," somebody to turn to during those difficult hours spent alone, when a person needs somebody to talk to.

The song concludes with a thrice-repeated variation of the chorus. The sentiment is poignant; the alienation is universal; the fantasy is escapist; the song is Americana! No doubt, the song helped John and The Zone enjoy some divine luck with their financial situations.

The fourth cut, called "Danger List," is an interesting self-analysis–type song. The speaker, in the chorus, says he does not seek affection. He is searching for self-assurance, for somebody he can love and respect. The speaker is a young man worrying about his self-concept and concerned about death. Cougar hits home: the speaker is every one of us. The speaker, even in the opening lines, confesses his need for a new direction (a new sunrise) from which to carve a new life, a new beginning. Sadly, the narrator is aware that straight women ignore him because he is too wild. Nevertheless, the speaker looks forward to changing his ways and developing a less threatening reputation. This "new sunrise" will resurrect him from a type of social death.

After the chorus, the young man mentions heaven and prayers. A silent man who says very little, the speaker still wants the Big Man (God) to care about him, to accept him as he is. Then the concluding stanza expresses the initiate's concept of heaven and home being synonymous. The speaker asks the Lord to fly him home to heaven because life on earth has made him so insecure. This unstable individual welcomes the opportunity to be with God, safely tucked away in a noncompetitive, nonjudgmental haven above.

Maybe this guy is confused and troubled, but he maintains communication with his God and we are hopeful that all will turn out fine for him. "Danger List" is not a great song of songs, but it is a young man's scrutinized introspection of himself. The number is also another illustration of how John Cougar Mellencamp writes about life's troubles and frustrations without making life seem unbearable and impossible. Troubled though he is, this young man symbolizes hope and redemption. He will survive—personifying Mellencamp's theme.

"Can You Take It?" is a brisk, luring change of pace: we live a fantasy. As usual, John's speaker is a young man. This is why so many speculate about whether John uses his songs to convey his personal experiences and inner thoughts. Many writers have had to tolerate these interesting speculations. This young man dates a beautiful southern belle with a wealthy father and a sports car. Sounds great! Then, she apparently invites him over one night, when her parents are away, asking if such an invitation prompts any ideas. It sounds unbelievable! They watch a little television and drink a little wine. Then, parting from her stereotyped role, she dominates the situation by claiming he is hers for the evening. He wonders if she is trying to make a fool out of him, as he recovers from his dismay. Then, she says the lines of the chorus to him, questioning if they really are going to "go all the way." How shocked he must have been to have this liberated young southern belle spew the same line to him that he had used on her earlier. Mr. Mellencamp seems to be having fun with us in this song. Then, capping the fantasy, John says to himself, ending the song with a note of joy, that even a jerk like him could sometimes be so unbelievably lucky.

The back side of the *American Fool* platinum album opens with "Thundering Hearts." Another fun-loving Mellencampish song, it opens with a memorable comical image. In order to cool off in the hot summer, these guys drive a Chevy convertible through a car wash. Great fun. A relaxed Cougar shows up here. Then, after devouring some french fries, the motorcycle-loving Mellencamp speaks proudly about his love of riding his Harley Davidson on a hot summer day. He picks up a Kentucky girl who knew him when he was just beginning his career. Mellencamp certainly conveys his love of this girl, as well as his love of the valley of the thundering hearts. Can there be any doubt about these lyrics being autobiographical? The protagonist yearns for the valley of the thundering hearts, where, later, he confesses that he would like to remain forever. What is or where is the valley of the thundering hearts? At the end of the number, the speaker (John, perchance) tells this Kentucky girl that night will soon arrive, cooling down the town. He hopes the two of them (John and Priscilla?) will remain "in the valley of the thundering hearts." Possibly, this valley, this substitute for heaven, this small town, is none other than Seymour, Indiana. This song is not particularly subtle, but a heartfelt tribute to John's hometown nevertheless.

Speculation leads me to believe that "Close Enough" is also autobiographical. The lyrics sound too much like the John Cougar/John Mellencamp we have grown to appreciate and understand—to some degree, anyway. Claiming to be a "backsliding fool" whenever anybody pushes him to walk in step with everybody else, he admits that he is not a pillar of the community, nor a person who has a respectable job or pals around with the right people. The female he addresses may believe herself to be superior to him, but he is "close enough" to his rock music to allow this love to compensate for his losing her.

Isn't this John Cougar Mellencamp—searching for his own identity in the town; searching for employment on his own terms; running with his true friends, even if others disapprove; trying to walk a straight line, but failing at the endeavor; thinking that others feel superior to him; pretending he doesn't care what others think? How memorable is that line about being a backsliding fool. What better verbiage to say he cannot survive on any terms other than being true to his own instincts and marching to his own drummer!

American Fool concludes with a more worldly, less personal account of loneliness. A slow, heart-rending narrative, "Weakest Moments" conveys the sympathy the male speaker possesses for the lady whose former lovers ("heroes") wonder if she is still alone. Why have permanence and commitment eluded this woman? The guy knows the lady fools around with her uncle and is aware that previous "flings" return periodically. But even the gentleman who purchased a diamond ring for her is leaving her. All she does, to handle her loss, is sunbathe. The faithful, loyal narrator, however, promises to be with her whenever she needs him. Even though her skin is oiled with the sweat of her lovers (what an appropriate metaphor), the compassionate narrator refuses to desert her, even during her "weakest moments."

The only other verse in this number mentions a former lover and talks about the dreams that circulate through her mind and body. Dreams that have died are another recurrent theme in the lyrics from the pen and mind of John Cougar Mellencamp. The speaker here is capable of sympathetic understanding and sincere concern. Unlike the young protagonist in "Danger List," for whom we optimistically harbor a real hope, the best happiness we can muster for this lady in "Weakest Moments" is a cautious reservation. Time is not going to be on her side much longer; also, we see no real attempt on her part to change. Loneliness and alienation, common themes in Cougar's lyrics, claim yet another victim—undeserving and innocent to some degree maybe, but void of fulfillment and contentment nevertheless. This is sad, indeed, but it is the nature of reality that circumstances sometimes gobble us up before we even truly define the problem. Once again, John shows the colors of a literary naturalist. Environmental determinism is a potent force.

One more entry appears on this chart-busting *American Fool* album. The second cut on the flip side, "China Girl," is the only song on the album that was not written by John Cougar Mellencamp. About a young man who tries to convince a Chinese girl that associating with him would not be sinful, the song is appropriately called "China Girl." It was written by Joe New and Jeff Silbar. Also, for "Hurt's So Good" and "Thundering Hearts," G. M. Green shares the honors of authorship. Zone guitarist Larry Crane shares the billing for "Danger List." No single individual is ever exclusively responsible for the success or the failure of a record album. John is fortunate enough and astute enough to know what he wants and to associate himself with talented, capable musicians who assist him with this delivery. This way, the delivered "baby" is healthy, strong, and appealing.

American Fool was not only an artistic triumph and financial breakthrough for John and The Zone. *American Fool* proved to be a dream come true, exhibiting the deserved rewards and providing the much-appreciated recognition of the hitherto overlooked and ignored musician and his band. Calling his own shots, to a large extent, John proved to many critics that he was not a mere "Little Bastard" who only relished in confronting others. John proved that his artistic ideas possessed merit, his creative endeavors possessed appeal, and his personal style possessed marketability. The decade-long struggle for professional recognition, John's dream of success, became a reality.

CHAPTER THIRTEEN

Uh-huh
Riva, 1983

The opening song of *Uh-huh*, as well as the first of three videos from the album, is the hard-to-define "Crumblin' Down." Watching John slide down the ladder, in the video, is a real thrill for my three-year-old. Almost a musical example of the stream-of-consciousness literary technique, the song is tough to pin down. From what John tells us, the song helped him to come to terms with his changing image and with the different treatment he was receiving after the phenomenal (and well-deserved) success of *American Fool*.

Lyrically, "Crumblin' Down" conveys a philosophy of life. In essence, it is that until one learns to bend the rules of society, he will not receive the best of anything. Some people are no good and untrustworthy, while others refuse to reward good deeds. The real world, the speaker feels, uses him as a "whipping boy," a sacrificial lamb who ultimately plays the scapegoat. Claiming he is not a sinner, he concedes that he has been the "whipping boy" for so long that he has adjusted to the reality. Then success hit. His critics were proven wrong. Newspapers print his pictures, along with informative articles, and everybody starts to treat him differently. But fame and fortune do not promise that the walls won't ever crumble and tumble, destroying everything. Even fame and fortune can be superficial and vulnerable triumphs.

What do these lyrics mean? Do they mean anything at all? George Green assisted with these lyrics; the lyrics present a series of quick, rapidly changing images that don't always directly relate to each other. Who are these people who are no good, who cannot be trusted, who punish good deeds? If we treat the song autobiographically, as John himself has implied that we should, these people are the businessmen who call the shots in the recording industry. These are the guys who place marketing above music. This means that the "whipping boy" is John himself. Time has taught him the importance of bending the rules; then changes began to occur.

With these changes, however, different problems lurk in the shadows. Newspapers carry pictures and articles about him. People—even some lifelong friends, perhaps—don't treat him like the Indiana greaser anymore. Everybody treats him differently. The succession of quick, stream-of-consciousness images keeps us alert to the lyrics. Some people still see the speaker (John?) as obnoxious and lazy, holding meaningless opinions because he is uneducated. Maybe John is obnoxious, but he can hardly be accused of laziness—at least not now. Yet the protagonist hangs onto that part of his identity that helps him cope with this dichotomy of dual images. Knowing he is a fine dancer and knowing what he is after work in harmony to provide the stabilizing element the speaker requires. Also hoped for is the stabilizing influence of a caring girl who will place her arms around him and breath into his ear. The speaker wants warmth, understanding, and the pursuit of his dreams. (He also wants to be turned on.) Yet, he realizes that the dream might shatter; he realizes that the walls might crumble and tumble. Life has its risks, to be sure. But this speaker seems to be chasing his fantasy and harnessing his dream. This is the Mellencamp touch: the theme that hope rings eternal, that hope is ever present, that people are entitled to contentment.

The second video from this album is my favorite. "Pink Houses" salutes small towns, but it also generates some questions about the entire concept of the American dream. The little pink houses, in essence, symbolize the embodiment of that American dream. An elderly black man apparently thinks he is set for life: he has his wife, his house, and his black cat. Is the cat a symbolic omen? But the guy has an interstate running through his yard. Is this the realization of the American dream? John, obviously, thinks not, but the elderly black gentleman is content. John's second example of the American dream being thwarted is a teenage male who wears a T-shirt and listens to a rock radio station. When he was younger, the boy was told he would be president. Now he thinks this futureless existence must be his final destination. Mellencamp emits sorrow and empathy for this young teenager, as well as for the elderly man: the dream has passed them over, coercing them into settling for something less than what they are theoretically entitled to in this land of opportunity.

One explanation for John's ability to convey the intensity of this loss lies embedded in his own background, with his personal struggle to succeed in a hotly competitive field. About the teenager, the lyrics sadly inform us that his hopes and dreams, like everything else, fade away into oblivion, becoming shelved memories from the past. John believes that an individual must possess the strength of character and confidence from within to fight to protect his dream. John also lives by this conviction, as we already realize. The final lines of "Pink Houses" contrast, however briefly, the concept of winners and losers, the successful and the unsuccessful. Herein, though, roosts a mature understanding of the American dream. Prior to adulthood, any observant individual realizes that we may all be created equally, but we are certainly not all equal. From one standpoint, the American dream is the birthchild of political propaganda, of capitalistic marketing, of promotional images. To the extent that we believe in the concept and the image that is perpetuated by the American dream, we will be socialized. But the horn of plenty is, unfortunately, not full enough to deal a winning hand to each and every person. Thus we are competitive. And when we compete for the rewards, some have a stronger arsenal of weaponry than others. This fact may not be fair, but we eventually realize that justice is not necessarily predicated on fairness.

Yet even with the inconsistencies, John doesn't forsake the

American dream. He does not give up on America and her people. I hope we will learn to keep the dream in proper perspective, but we also need to keep striving for the realization of that dream. The pink house is a representation of that dream. For that black man, the house with the interstate nearby was just fine. This man is satisfied with what he reaped from the horn of plenty, so we should accept that. The teenager will probably never be president, but on the other hand, he does not have to lackadaisically accept his present condition as his final destination. Thus we are pleased that the black man is content and we are hopeful for the teenager to redfine his dream so he can rejuvenate his spirit. John Cougar Mellencamp likes both of these poeple and wants us to accept the "different strokes for different folks" viewpoint.

"Pink Houses" is a song that makes us feel decent about ourselves. The lyrics are not directly patriotic, nor are they dripping with sentimental dribble. But the lyrics do convey love and hope, individualism and naturalism, competition and success. Isn't this what the Founding Fathers wanted America to represent? Perhaps the chorus of "Pink Houses" expresses these varied feelings best: Mellencamp sees America as a political statement, as she offers both freedom and little pink houses to everyone, yet she is something worth seeing because the concepts of success and survival conjure up such diversified images to different people.

Bitterness and aggression are nonexistent in these words. True, America is not always what she appears to be. True, America cannot be everything to everybody. But Americans are survivors. Americans are dreamers. Americans believe in the pink houses. John Mellencamp did. He is doing fine, by almost any barometer that somebody might care to use as a gauge. I tip my hat to John for writing such a song.

"Authority Song" is the third video from the *Uh-huh* album. One night inquire as to why a then–thirty-two-year old would write and sing about fighting authority. The video finds John in a boxing ring, where, he claims, he did not feel comfortable. The original idea for the video was to show film clips of various confrontations with authority. But editing and deciphering the many possible choices became such a time-consuming hurdle that the idea was abandoned. Although John claims to be satisfied with the final results of the boxing-ring video, this version is vastly different from the original concept. John fondly refers to the young boy in the video as his alter ego. The boy is surrounded, as John is, by various symbols of military, financial, and/or domestic authority: officers, businessmen, adults. The "Authority Song" video is popular, as would be any video from Mellencamp, but I find myself curiously yearning to see an "Authority Song" video based upon the initial, historical overview of famous confrontations with authority.

In the chorus, the lyrics concede that authority always wins. The juvenile speaker is proud of his willingness to challenge authority, even though we are uninformed about the issues he is challenging. Nevertheless, we admire the lad and trust that the issues are meaningful enough to warrant the confrontations. In his personal life, John has been pleased with his willingness to battle issues he thought were wrong. And John has certainly experienced his share of battles with the so-called establishment. Even as an adolescent, John suggests he was this way. So, once again, we tend to scrutinize the lyrics from an autobiographical perspective.

Sophomorically, Mr. Mellencamp becomes a bit twofaced and hypocritical in his lyrics to "Authority Song." Of course, adolescents who see themselves as being forced by the establishment to compromise their beliefs will agree with John that such treatment is a disgrace to the dignity of the individual victim. Teens will identify and empathize with the picture John composes. Here, the narrator/victim asks the minister for the strength to endure more fighting, but the wise minister tells the lad he needs maturity, not strength. But the manchild responds, revealing his fear of growing old. Maturity carries us closer to old age, to dying. He loves life, as indeed he should, yet he fears death, which is unfortunate. Fans will tend to view the boxing-ring setting, plus the chorus of this song, as an admonition to confront authority, even though one must realize he will lose the battle. Why does the narrator chronically grin over his defeats at challenging authority? Why does the narrator never win his confrontations? Is the narrator living a "rebel without a cause" syndrome? The dialogue in the lyrics is effective, yet the lyrics lose their dynamic impact because any significant moral is too elusive to define. Of course, rock-and-roll lyrics operate on no formula that promises a logical thematic concept. "Authority Song" is a fun song, no doubt, but isn't Mellencamp now the authority figure who has proven himself, who calls the shots? Isn't the rock star projecting a hypocrisy when he markets a video that attacks authority for no definite reason, without even defining what the "authority" happens to be? Unfortunately, this song and its popular video are apparently designed to hype the media image of the rebel star. This is not all so terrible, but the marketing tool would be more effective if it did not blur the point of the lyrics.

Another light entertainment-oriented excursion to our adolescence, where life seemed intimidating at times, yet worthwhile—that is "Authority Song." Why, however, did John suddenly begin to add punctuation and quotation marks to the printed lyrics on the record sleeve? In the chorus, why is the *comma* that follows "authority" changed to a *period* in the repeated line that follows the emotional series of "oh no"? Why, also, did a youngster who is battling authority turn to the preacher for solace? Obviously, the lad does not see the minister as a threat in this particular encounter. Who is the "they" who force the kid into a compromising position, then smile? Would a teacher do this? A parent? Many variables enter into an answer for such a question as this. Perhaps John experienced this type of physical intimidation as a means of coercion when he was younger. But in the decade of the eighties, a reasonably stable and emotionally secure adult authority figure—whether parent, teacher, or whoever—would not utilize this brand of exerting authority. The personification of "Authority," in the chorus, which explains the capitalization of "A," is a laudable poetic technique. Personification serves a dual function: it clears the way for dialogue, which clears the road to understanding and grasping the theme.

What actually is the thematic significance of "Authority Song"? In 1985, teenagers are becoming more conservative and more oriented toward locating solvent employment, establishing domestic stability, and creating personal satisfaction than was common during the sixties and seventies. Why does John seem to write a song that addresses a more rebellious, less conservative person—say, from the decade of the sixties or seventies, for example? John misleads us, in my opinion, with the title of this popular tune. Instead of encouraging teens to fight authority (after all, he always lost), John possibly wants adolescents to realize that life is a changing process. Whatever seems important now may not be important next year. In addition, authority comes wrapped in different packages. In the chorus, John himself turns to the preacher, a moral/spiritual authority, seeking strength. The minister explains that the necessary ingredient to face life and its reality is not so much that of strength. Maturity is what John lacks.

Then, when the speaker is told that he needs to grow up, we learn what the real problem is. The lad is not worried about authority, at least not authority per se, since he does not reject all forms of authority. The young boy—John himself hitting us with his role of being Everyboy—fears growing up because he fears death. He rejects adulthood because he sees it as being closer to death. The title of "Authority Song" is misleading, because it directs attention to a stereotyped authority. The real authority problem for this boy/man is his ever active mind, which causes him to ponder the essence of existence. This is scary. So he fights the answers. Time, however, shows that his real fears are unnecessary; hence, his mind, his Authority, always wins the battles. But the personified Authority, rather than being an external persona, is an internal entity. "Authority Song," being mislabled, confuses the reader—it is common and simplistic, on one hand; symbolic and perceptive, on the other. But, true to the style of John Cougar Mellencamp, the song possesses a magical appeal on any and all levels of interpretation. That heartstring of universal humanness has been strummed once again.

The fourth cut, written in collaboration with George Green, is called "Warmer Place to Sleep." Biblical allusions and symbolism saturate this unusual composition. The speaker has been to the mountain and witnessed the ashes (sin, ruination) below; he has shared breakfast with "the wiseman" (Christ), who has enlightened him with knowledge; he has slept with Jezebel; he has seen the heart of darkness; he has been called both Abel and Cain by the voice (conscience, spirit) out in the desert; he has slept in the rain (redemption, rebirth) for forty days and forty nights; he has rested in the devil's arms and chased the hounds of hell; he has fraternized with the angels and has learned that hearts are equal. This is one busy agenda! But the figurative language is poetically manipulated to reveal this protagonist's hunger for experiences, thirst for knowledge, and quest for self-revelation. All of the metaphors and symbolism aside, what the speaker yearns for is simple human warmth (company, compassion). The tone of the song is one of stark directness and simple truth. The pace moves right along with an aggressive, yet non-threatening speed.

Surprisingly, in the lyrics, Mellencamp is willing to trade his ambitions for a warm bed. But can John Cougar really be serious about suggesting that anything can take priority over a person's ambitions, his dreams? John Cougar has perpetually and diligently worked to make his personal dream a reality. For Mellencamp, his dream has been his identity. Thus, sleep (the warm bed) offers him the chance to think and reflect and define that self-esteem, that dream. Amen. Dreams and ambitions are the food of life. And nobody would say, a la Mame, that John Cougar Mellencamp is not partaking of the banquet. On the other hand, dignity, honesty, and identity must never be lost during the feast. The final chorus of the song asks the girl if he could seek sanctuary (retreat) from life in her warm bed, where he can avoid facing the truth. Don't mistakingly judge this as sexual lust; the "safe retreat" is an escape where neither he (in the first chorus, this *I* is *they*) nor anybody else can look into his eyes. The eyes are that magical key to open that door to all introspection and understanding. As of yet, the speaker is not ready for that. Now the confused and frightened protagonist seeks retreat, not confrontation. He needs to reconnoiter for another charge. "Warmer Place to Sleep," to me, is a thought-provoking lesson in self-realization and becoming of age. What at first glance appears to be a "boy wants into girl's bed" type of chorus is actually, when viewed in context, a "boy wants to conquer himself" plea.

"Jackie O," written with John Prine, needs explanation. The speaker is addressing a person who attended a party with Jackie Onassis. Hence the song's title. But the speaker accuses this person of not being able to see (because of not wearing glasses) the harm being done to him, the speaker. The glasses symbolize some crystal ball, as these glasses will help this person to look ahead into the future, to see tomorrow. (Would you *really* want to have such a pair of glasses?) The speaker also projects a degree of paranoia. The speaker has heard this other person cussing and has seen this person talking to his second cousin. This communication threatens the speaker, as he fears this person and the second cousin were talking about him. Then the speaker wants this other person to acquire backstage passes from the politically powerful father, an intriguing father-figure metaphor. But the speaker wonders why this person cannot dance better. The speaker, alas, sees dancing in terms of power, and power allows action. Even in "Crumblin' Down," John refers to dancing as an avenue of combating criticism and of accepting reality. A similar sequence of thoughts is scattered throughout "Jackie O."

Music as a psychological defense mechanism, almost equivalent to an aphrodisiac, is the theme of "Play Guitar." This light-spirited, fun song was composed in conjunction with Dan Ross and Larry Crane, a guitarist in The Zone. Rather than being an instrument of defeat and destruction, music is, for many, a tool of establishing identity and creating status. The speaker says, in the opening lines, that learning to play guitar is the most effective method of tasting success. New cars, trendy haircuts, cushy jobs, and even dating cheerleaders are fine, but they won't automatically endow one with "success." The final stanza challenges one who seeks success. Here John and The Zone must be really laughing at themselves, in this playful, energy-packed song. Rather than being taken seriously, the guys are poking fun at themselves and delighting in the process. To be successful, the lyrics tell us, play the guitar. All the "macho shit" can be forgotten about. Pumping iron, dressing up, cruising the streets, and scoring nightly are all fine. But, the song says, women desire a "phony rock star" who strums the guitar; all else is secondary.

Oh, the omnipotence of guitar playing! What a panacea for all problems—sociological, occupational, recreational, and even psychological. Not to be taken literally, no doubt, "Play Guitar" does carry the message that doing such will reduce our vulnerability while, at the same time, it will enhance our confidence and self-esteem. The lyrics are humorous, yet serious. So playing guitar is seen in a positive light, instead of being cast as a lazy, downtrodden, leisurely pursuit.

The third cut on the reverse side, "Serious Business," uses the television technique of passing a quick succession of images before the listener. Girls and boys are at a pool, having fun, yet the tone is rather somber. The speaker seems to be fleeing some unnamed fear, which creates an aura of mysteriousness and deception. The lyrics of the chorus sound like a battle cry. Sex, violence, and rock and roll are serious business. The last stanza, however, is by far the most uneasy. Mellencamp asks to be hung on a cross, so everybody can view him. With him a crucified figure, void of life and soul, with his name hanging around his neck, people can continue to throw stones at him.

What a downer image: John Cougar Mellencamp hanging on a cross, as a sacrificial lamb who has given up. So unlike the artist, this departure seems increasingly disturbing. True, being a successful rock star is serious business—financially lucrative, creatively challenging, personally draining. The final verse here shows the worst that could happen. More likely, a perceptive rock star would have the insight to quit while he was ahead, rather than to be destroyed by his adoring public.

"Lovin' Mother fo Ya," the combined effort of John Cougar

and Will Cary, contains two unique metaphors. First, in the opening stanza, the authors describe a man/boy riding through the park on his motorcycle, which is described as a stallion. Wearing a golden tan and a devil-man tattoo, the man-boy rides his chrome-and-steel stallion through the Park, feeling quite real. Sitting atop this cycle, probably a Harley Davidson, gives this man/boy all the recognition he needs. His identity is inseparable from the bike. The third and final stanza reveals this individual's vulnerability. The man/boy asks his girl to squeeze him tightly so he doesn't collapse. To feel like a man, the boy wants his "kickin' mule" to go "into her stall." Rarely does such a vivid, appropriate metaphor emerge to describe the insertion of a penis ("kickin' mule") into a vagina ("stall"). Not a tender, passionate metaphor, to be sure, but it conveys the urgency of the speaker. He does not want to discover love; he wants to assert manliness. Perhaps this man/boy is actually a boy/man, lodging his brains in his genitals.

Unfortunately, "Golden Gates," the last song on the *Uh-huh* album, was never made into a video. The sentiments portray a John Cougar Mellencamp who salutes and praises the basic, simple human values that provide each of us with the stamina and the drive to endure and prevail. John says this song expresses what he believes to be the real John Mellencamp. This revelation hits us as a surprise. Assuming it to be true, why, then, does John continue to perpetuate this macho image of drinking, fighting, and romancing? Even on this album, he reenforces this rogue image with such songs as "Serious Business" and "Lovin' Mother fo Ya." The kid inside, apparently, has trouble staying in touch with the reality of the various images. John Cougar/John Mellencamp suffers from an identity crisis, yet as he matures and mellows, he is becoming more successful at overcoming himself. Even the sincere honesty that saturates the lyrics of "Golden Gates" reflects this confused growth.

Success has, we have seen, been kind to John Mellencamp. Since he has justified his existence and pacified his ego, Mellencamp is exposing his vulnerability while dropping the media-hyped image of the macho stud. Songs like "Golden Gates," nevertheless, introduce us to a mellower John Cougar Mellencamp. Golden gates and pearled streets and friendly angels don't exist in the real world. Uncertain futures and big business do exist. But Mellencamp is tired of seeing deals going down, lonely men, crying women, pimps and prostitutes, and other such seamy realities. Authorities, he says, leave us on our own, so he (Mellencamp) needs this lover to give him the strength to endure and to survive. Together, their promises from the heart will create their own "golden gates."

Poetically, the structure of this song is interesting. The first stanza, twelve lines, is the longest. The golden gates, the pearled streets, and the singing angels certainly entice and lure us, causing our romantic wonderlust and escapist dreams. Then the romantic dream merges into realistic naturalism: uncertain futures, dealing masters (bosses and so on), and personal alienation. Then romantic escapism returns. He wants a suite that overlooks the Park, a place of eternal beauty and spiritual rejuvenation. And, within the private confines of that suite, the pair will share their promises and their truths as their hearts become one.

Then arriveth reality, in the second stanza, which is four lines shorter than the first. Here the protagonist/speaker (John?) announces that he has already seen enough deals fall apart, enough lonely people, and enough prositiues yearning for redemption. He desperately wants to call for reservations at this dreamlike suite by the Park. But reality and its troubles tax the emotional range he exists in. Yet, all the pain and anger aside, he harnesses and defines his desires and knows he wants out of the dark unknown.

The concluding stanza, shorter yet, with only five lines, conveys one of the themes of "Golden Gates." We must realize that nobody is going to intervene on our behalf, taking care of our problems. By the same token, even after realizing we are essentially on our own, we possess a human need to find somebody whom we can trust and in whom we can confide. Ironically, even though we are on our own, we are not islands unto ourselves. The protagonist openly confides his inner conviction and fear that he lacks the necessary strength to accomplish what he wants with his life. Thus he searches for a trusting confidante—his golden gate—to assist with the creation of this strength. In my opinion, a video of "Golden Gates" would have been a successful venture, as well as provided a new twist. "Golden Gates" and "Pink Houses" are my two favorites on the *Uh-huh* album.

The diversity of emotions that John Cougar Mellencamp is able to express in his lyrics is one source of the strength of his songs. This quiet, unassuming power is evident on the *Uh-huh* album. At times, John projects a cocky toughness; at other times, he is confidently tame. Sometimes he is apple pie, while later he is evil sex. At times, he is a sexy and self-examining James Dean; then he can become a flamboyant, aggressive punk. Yet John Cougar Mellencamp is able to do this because he is fortunate enough to own a sixth sense. This endowment allows him to split the fine line between commanding and controlling the song without dominating and destroying the messages contained therein.

One reason John can do this is because—with some songs, at least—he is apparently writing about his own past and his own attitudes and feelings. But this autobiographical tendency is merely part of the gift. John is capable of splitting this fine line because he is capable of understanding and identifying with numerous situations and a diversity of people. This sympathetic love and unpredictable mysteriousness combine to create a tremendous musical force in the rock and roll that John Cougar Mellencamp writes, sings, and performs.

As an artist, as a musician, as a businessman, and as an entertainer, John should be proud of the *Uh-huh* album, which took two years to complete. The acoustics of "Crumblin' Down" and "Pink Houses," the high-stepping drumming, the energetic humanizing, and the enthusiastic dynamics blend into a workable symbiosis that delivers the strengths and the weaknesses of the heartland of America: Mellencamp country, in Indiana. Another triumph of *Uh-huh*—besides its versatility, poignancy, honesty, and passion—is its dedication to the Rolling Stones.

The record sleeve proudly salutes the Stones with the accolade of special thanks: "To the Rolling Stones for never takin' the livin' room off the records when we were kids." Like the Stones, John prides himself on writing about and singing about the people, places, and problems he understands.

CHAPTER FOURTEEN

Scarecrow
Riva, 1985

Driving on East State Road 46 in Bloomington, Indiana, one stumbles upon an elaborate and decorative fence. An eye-catcher, the wooden fence, with its brick abutment and iron gate, suggests an out-of-the-ordinary residence on this heavily traveled two-lane road. Behind these portals, nestled amongst the trees that adorn the wooded acreage, is the residence of John Cougar Mellencamp. As one presses the security button, the eye of the camera focuses in on the visitor, already tense, merely to be outside the home of John Cougar Mellencamp. The camera's probing eye and its impersonal stare add to the nervous jitters that already make one's stomach uneasy.

With the media image Mellencamp has fostered over the previous years, some people are shocked that such an authority-fighting rebel has funneled so much money into creating such a womblike security blanket. This costly, yet unfriendly fence greets one with the admonition to stay away, not with a warm welcome. On the other hand, those who expect Johnny Cougar to live in a $70,000 two-story home located in a typical subdivision do not understand the difference between the media image and the real man. Even though the Mellencamps' abode is equipped with an indoor pool, tennis courts, a gazebo, a satellite dish, and Corvettes, the residence is somewhat modest and homey, especially when compared to the grossly opulent homes of certain other rock personalities.

John's egotistical, flippant temper has sometimes taken a hold of him in the past. But the image is changing. His publicity agent, the Howard Bloom Organization, undoubtedly hopes that the outbursts such as those with Felicia Jeter and with the Ontario concert come to an abrupt halt. The task is to revamp the image. John Cougar Mellencamp—a thirty-four–year–old father of three daughters, as well as a potent force in contemporary music—has been examining his own behavior and attitudes, defining where he wants to go with his career. (John's oldest daughter was parented by Priscilla. Vicki, his current wife, delivered their second daughter, a five-pound–three-ounce bundle named Rickie Lee, on August 14, 1985.) Already a rich man who, by his own admission, would never ever have to work another day in his life, John Mellencamp wants to direct his energies toward creating a meaningful impact on the music world and his fans. The manchild is struggling to become a seasoned professional.

Against this background, John's eighth record album, called *Scarecrow*, was released. The first single, "Lonely Ol' Night," backed with "The Kind of Fella I Am," is evidence that Johnny Cougar is, indeed, growing up and accepting his role as a rock star. Nearly two years has passed since *Uh-Huh* was released; logic would indicate that much has been learned during this period. Much has transpired, to be sure. On MTV, in June of 1985, John spoke about the responsibility of a rock star to realize that what he says does have an impact on fans, including adolescents. Unashamedly, John has made an about-face, admitting that a rock performer should direct a responsive look at the fans who place so much meaning in the lyrics of their favorite star. But rock stars in general seem to be more cognizant of their impact. The Live Aid benefit for starving Ethiopians is the most obvious example of the rock world harnessing its collective powers to become a potent political and financial agent for change.

As of this writing, John has just completed working with Willie Nelson to organize a benefit for farmers, aptly referred to as Farm Aid. (This particular chapter was written old full year after the other chapters of the book.) Tentative plans called for giants such as Bob Dylan, Hall and Oates, Neal Young, and Rickie Lee Jones to lend their voices and their appeal to the cause. Steve Perry, originally booked to appear, was forced to cancel, due to other commitments. The concert was scheduled for September 22, 1985, at Memorial Stadium at the University of Illinois. Tickets—90,000 of them—were sold for $17.50. (By the time this book is published, this concert will be part of rock 'n' roll history.) The point, however, is that John has matured and mellowed, realizing that even an average student from the Indiana heartland can organize a worthwhile project, lend his famous name to a laudable cause, and direct attention toward an unfortunate reality—in this case, the plight of the farmer.

The *Scarecrow* album was recorded at Belmont Mall, a complete and modern twenty-four–track studio that was the brainchild of John himself. Located near Bloomington, Belmont Mall is a state-of-the-art studio that even impresses Don Gehman, who has worked with John and co-produced some of his former albums. Plans are in the works to allow new, young, aspiring bands to use Belmont Mall for a much smaller fee that would be charged for other studios. A tour is being planned for the fall of 1985, according to the newsletter that is sent to the members of the recently organized John Cougar Mellencamp Fan Club. Aside from the tour and the new recording studio, which was completed in March 1985, John is thrilled about the *Scarecrow* album, as he is making actual statements in his lyrics, rather than being "cute" as in the famous refrain of "Jack and Diane."

The February, 1986, issue of *Playboy*, in fact, will highlight a key interview with John, where he will candidly discuss his career, the *Scarecrow* album, and other plans and activities. As of this writing, the issue of *Playboy* is not yet on the newsstand shelves, but the feature interview is bound to be more upbeat and satisfying than the interview that appeared in the August 1985 issue of *Penthouse*. Inside sources clandestinely reveal that John is not particularly proud of the *Penthouse* interview, as he regrets saying some of the things he said. Sometimes a backsliding innocent, even when it comes to his own image polishing,

John speaks in the interview about his father's sexual entanglement with one of his teachers while he was still in high school; about how his father met his mother while escaping the police on the streets of Austin, Indiana, after a Saturday-afternoon fight; about Larry's wife, Nancy, and her adolescent decision-making conflicts over alcohol, joints, and the Nazarene church; about John's being the first student at Seymour High School to be busted by a narcotics agent for drug abuse; of his first marriage to a University of Michigan coed, Priscilla, and his willingness to let her support him; of his senseless encounters with death, using a pickup truck and a welded steel cage chained onto the bumper; about the loss of his high-school class ring, making a sentimental loss a rather crude story; about constantly fighting to win a girl; and a few closing remarks about what would ultimately become the *Scarecrow* album.

Allegedly, the *Penthouse* interview was held on a tour bus. Regardless, loyal fans must remain hopeful that this kind of self-satisfying grandstanding will cease. Mellencamp should avoid this type of interview, which concentrates upon the macho bravado of his past, and steer toward interviews that deal honestly and openly with his talent, his career, his love of music, and his fans. Once again, however, John's fine blend of arrogance and innocence, coupled with his zeal for good fun and his love of sheer con, have surged foward, pushing his talent onto the back burner. John gains confidence in himself when he meets others on his own terms. David Alvin, of the Blasters, for example, can now be added to the growing list of musicians, such as Mitch Ryder, who kowtow to John's professional knowledge and musical talent. Diligently, John assisted the Blasters with the merchandising of their *Hard Line* album. In actuality, David Alvin defers to John, admitting that John essentially wrote and produced "Colored Lights." John, who, like all of us, finds it frustrating to speak about his own talents without sounding pompous, must develop the ability to do just that: to comfortably and convincingly cope with the strengths and the weaknesses of his personal talent. When John overcomes his feelings of inferiority and learns to talk to interviewers without feeling threatened and intimidated, interviews such as the one in *Penthouse* will cease. Then fans will hear and read more about John's talent and his career and his family, not his macho deportment, his fighting authority, and his substance abuse. The new image of skill and confidence is overcoming the former image of women, booze, sex, and fighting. Every kid grows up, including John Mellencamp.

Stare at the cover of the *Scarecrow* album or at the picture sleeve of the "Lonely Ol' Night" single. The transformation is jelling into a more concrete, more noticeable form. Physically, John is clean-shaven, with a rustic, yet neater appearance. Even the trademark Marlboro doesn't hang from his lips. He seems shy and introspective, instead of macho and sexy. His personal magnetism catches the eye, downplaying the hyperbolic absurdity of his innocence and exploiting the commercial enterprise of his youthful handsomeness, his musical stature, his personal growth, and his synergistic relationship with those around him, including his devoted fans and his three daughters.

The opening song on side 1, titled "Rain on the Scarecrow," chronicles the plight of the modern farmer in the United States. This entry also provides John's new album release with its title. The scarecrow is a symbol of the farm, the nation's food supply. Yet the lyrics of this narrative poem tell a disastrous, yet all-too-common tale. The four-hundred–acre farm is being auctioned, as last summer's crops generated insufficient funds to pay off the loans. The speaker—John himself—remembers when he was only five years old, walking hand in hand with his grandfather, the hardworking man who had originally cleared the land. But the young speaker has lost more than those precious memories shared with his grandfather. He has also lost his dignity and his dream. His grandmother sits on the porch swing, clutching a Bible, praying for her entry into the Promised Land. The distraught grandson offers a prayer for the soul of the auctioneer, who has stepped in now that the Farmer's Bank has foreclosed. Narrator John counts the ninety-seven crosses, representing the ninety-seven families who have lost their farms. With the memories and the dreams shattered, he admits that he, too, feels like dying. He will have no farm to pass on to his son; only the symbolic blood of all farmers remains on the plow while the rain falls upon the scarecrow. The tearful raindrops offer little, if any, hope for redemption. The land that once made the speaker proud is being sold, auctioned away from the family after three generations of laborious effort and heartfelt love.

John Mellencamp's grandfather was a farmer; thus this song must be somewhat autobiographical. The *Scarecrow* album, along with *A Biography*, in 1978, is dedicated to John's grandfather. Harry (Speck) Mellencamp had a tremendous impact upon his loving and devoted grandson. Speck listened to John; he served as a father substitute, tolerating John's adolescent hotheadedness and foul language. John's grandfather died soon after Christmas Day in 1983. But the legacy of pride and dignity that Harry Mellencamp passed on to young John Mellencamp is a treasure that the maturing grandson is increasingly able to understand. On the inside record jacket, where the dedication of the album is found, fans also see a brief tribute to John's grandfather. With mixed emotions and sincere sympathy, John states: "There is nothing more sad or glorious than generations changing hands."

"Rain on the Scarecrow" was recorded March 29, 1985. But two days earlier, John's grandmother recorded her rendition of "Grandmas's Theme." Laura Mellencamp, Harry's widow, continues to reside in Seymour, Indiana, next door to her son Joe and close to John's father, Richard. On March 27, Laura Mellencamp sang a song that would ultimately follow "Rain on the Scarecrow" on her grandson's new album. No doubt, Harry would be pleased to witness John's continued success in the music world. He would also be proud to know about the Farm Aid concert scheduled for September 1985. Quite possibly, Harry Mellencamp went to his grave not fully comprehending the intensity of the impact he had upon his grandson. *Scarecrow*, John's first album release since his grandfather's death, salutes the memory of Harry Mellencamp and symbolizes the love and devotion that passed through these two individuals, a love that transcends our earthly boundaries.

John Mellencamp is also coming to terms with his real feelings toward small towns. Unlike the lyrics from previous songs, namely "Chestnut Street Incident" and "Dream Killin' Town," from John's first album, in 1976, *Scarecrow* introduces a number called "Small Town." Autobiographically chronicling his own boyhood, John says he was born and raised in a small town. In all probability, he says, he will die and be buried in a small town. His friends and parents also hail from small towns. Perhaps these small communities do limit opportunities, as his angry attacks against such places revealed in previous songs. But the hayseed narrator realized that his roots are in the small town; because he can be himself in the small town, he applauds the small town and proudly confesses that he is another boring romantic. These lyrics offer quite a revealing insight into John's personal self-concept and add credence to speculations made a year ago, in other chapters of this biographical profile.

The next three entries on side 1 deal with the enduring, yet popular, theme of loneliness. First, in "Minutes to Memories," the populist Mellencamp relates the story of a seventy-seven–year–old steelworker talking to a young man sitting beside him on a Greyhound bus. The elderly man is worn out, but is proud of his hardworking past in the steel mills of Gary, Indiana. Metaphorically, John sings about the long highway of life and about the honest old man's peace of mind being his pillow. The young man, looking back on the encounter with the lonely old man, realizes that the wisdom of the old man is the same knowledge that the young man will soon offer to his own son. Metaphorically and symbolically, "Minutes to Memories" is a unique song, as time seems to turn upon us. Days become minutes and minutes become memories, laments the chorus. The young at heart, representing the future, must hang in there and become the best they possibly can. The realities of life frequently create an alienation between us, a loneliness that is tough to define. But a certain existential singularity unites us, once we reach out to each other. Like Billy Joel's recent antisuicide video, reminding us that we are only human and prone to making mistakes, Mellencamp's lyrics also urge us to toughen up, to travel that long highway, and to leave a positive mark by accomplishing something worthwhile. The macho rebel, self-indulging himself with women and booze, has matured considerably!

Two other melodies deal with loneliness, albeit in a different light. "Lonely Ol' Night" relates the loneliness and fears of two young lovers attempting to reconcile their hopeful dreams with the frustrating reality of their lives. The video was shot in black and white, reminding the viewer of an old movie. Shot in southern Indiana, the video captures a little of each of us. The carnival background, coupled with the symbolism of the black-and-white photography, adds to the realism of the emotions felt by these two lovers. A third look at loneliness enters with "The Face of the Nation," which was recorded at Belmont Mall on April 19, 1985. The protagonist grapples with the loneliness inflicted upon him from the constant change he sees around him. He regrets the feelings of loneliness that emerge from his helplessness. Numerous lonely people are being defeated with destroyed dreams; the idealistic protagonist cannot recognize his own country any longer, because its face keeps changing so rapidly. Hopefully, however, the youth vows to continue his battle to improve things, at least for his lady and himself. This fight is for a purpose; thus Mellencamp's admonition to keep on trying is admirable and healthy.

The flip side of *Scarecrow* opens with an allegorical metaphor, "Justice and Independence '85." Independence Day was so named because he was born on July Fourth; eventually, Independence Day married a woman named Justice and they delivered a son named Nation. Then Mother Justice deserted her husband, who endured with the dream that he (Independence) and Justice and Nation would reunite. Justice insisted upon isolating herself, so Nation mourned and cried. Nation matured, running around and earning himself a reputation. Independence and Justice were ashamed of Nation's behavior. At first, they quarreled about who was to blame for Nation's attitude, but finally Independence and Justice agreed to reunite the family into a happy unit. Independence and Justice would try to make Nation secure and comfortable, so as to prevent his embarrassment. Compared with the lyrics of John Mellencamp's earlier works, these lyrics are a strong political statement, questioning the direction that our nation is heading while also hoping that justice will return to our social order. Mellencamp has not lost his ability to turn over a fine metaphor.

Lost dreams and enduring hope are the twin themes of "Between a Laugh and a Tear." The speaker is disillusioned over his feelings of emptiness and downheartedness. Without friends, forgetting about both the future and the past; the initiate discovers that his paradise no longer entertains him. Hence he has to smile at himself, walking the tightrope between a laugh and a tear. Although this song is not as upbeat as the others, it is, nevertheless, a hopeful tune in that it encourages one to advance a step at a time. This same optimistic love of life is evident in "Rumbleseat." Here the narrator is living in his hometown, feeling sorry for himself and for the world. He fears a nervous breakdown, but has no faith in psychiatrists. Drunkenness is a possible escape, but he rejects that answer, too. The chorus, on an upbeat swing, takes him to a fantasy dream where he rides along in the rumbleseat, symbolically being Numero Uno. On a positive note, the last verse sees the protagonist making an important decision. Since tomorrow offers him another chance, he promises that he will cease his self-criticism and make something out of his life. Riding in the rumbleseat, with his feet propped up, he will prove to himself and to others that he has turned his life in a new direction. Can there be any doubt that John Cougar Mellencamp, at age thirty-four, now finds himself riding high in the rumbleseat? Both "Rumbleseat" and "Between a Laugh and a Tear" are people songs, addressing feelings of hope and despair that we all have experienced. Both songs also possess hopeful lyrics, in that the young initiate is determined to be a winner, a success in his own way. Mellencamp's populist appeal and democratic thinking have struck home once again.

"You've Got to Stand for Somethin' " provides a fine lead-in to the last entry on the album, "R.O.C.K. in the U.S.A.," a salute to the rock of the sixties. If one does not stand for something, he will fall for anything, warns John. He has seen many things and knows many things, but admits that he has not seen everything and does not know everything. He has seen the Rolling Stones, the Who (in 1969), Marlon Brando on a motorcycle, and Sylvester Stallone as the Italian Stallion. He saw Khrushchev kissing Castro, astronauts on the moon, Miss America in a girlie magazine, and places like Harlan County; Paris, Texas; and Rome, Georgia. But he is proud to claim the Midwest as his home. The lyrics are a series of images suggesting the cultural reality of modern America. Unless we begin to respect and commit ourselves to certain goals and objectives, the world might smite our faces in revenge. The cultural turmoil, where one can rarely distinguish the real from the superficial, is dangerous.

Yet the *Scarecrow* album does not conclude with such a dire warning. "R.O.C.K. in the U.S.A." is a tribute to those musicians of the sixties who left their hometowns, carrying guitars and drums, hoping to make their dreams come alive. Blind faith kept them going: Frankie Lyman, Bobby Fuller, Mitch Ryder, Jackie Wilson, the Shangri-las, the Young Rascals, Martha Reeves, and, of course, one of Mellencamp's favorites, James Brown. As an adolescent, young John Mellencamp must have hearkened to the same yearning that these stars beckoned toward. Sure, they sought fame and wealth, but they also sought acceptance and justification.

The *Scarecrow* album contains eight songs written by John himself, two others that John coauthored with George M. Green, and the song sung by Laura Mellencamp, which is part of the public domain. More significant, however, is the fact that the Zone and John have continued to grow together, to nurture their symbiotic relationship. The aggressive hostility and juvenile frustration found in some of the earlier lyrics are being replaced by a more stable and confident understanding of reality.

Understanding reality, however, does not mean that we never try to alter it. This eternal hope in the individual and in his ability to effect change is one of the basic themes permeating *Scarecrow*. Regardless of how lonely one becomes or of how desperate a situation seems, faith and hope are never dead. This love of life, even when our dreams are being shattered, proves to be a constant, recurring theme in the lyrics of John Mellencamp. *Scarecrow* is an album that John and the Zone can be proud of; hopefully, sales will reward John's laudable attempt to say something meaningful in his lyrics. As a writer, as a musician, and as a man, John Mellencamp is coming of age. Musically, *Scarecrow* is a better album than *American Fool* and *Uh-Huh*. Commercially, the jury (the buying public) is still out.

Regardless of how consumers react to *Scarecrow*, fans will realize that rock-and-roll stardom continues to be a powerful aphrodisiac in John Mellencamp's life. Besides the financial affluence and the psychological identity, success as a rock performer has blessed John Mellencamp with a domestic compatability, where he accepts his responsibilities, and a social conscience, where he stands by his convictions. He did, for example, refuse permission for Ronald Reagan to use "Pink Houses" as a theme song for the 1984 reelection trail. Also, after hearing *Scarecrow*, some will question the wisdom of releasing an album that is not intentionally streamlined for commercial exploitation. On two occasions, then, Mellencamp has stuck by his personal standards and done the opposite of what one would expect a profiteer to do.

Perhaps John strives a little too much for meaningful relevance with some numbers on the *Scarecrow* album, but rock-and-roll stars who enter the arena with a political message have normally downplayed any sharp attacks. After all, the real protest decade has passed; perhaps a new one will surface, but contemporary performers tend to criticize through implication without suggesting a solution. "Justice and Independence '85" and "You've Got to Stand for Somethin' " are two such songs. Mellencamp continues, also, to forget that many fans would not see Bloomington, Indiana—or even Seymour, for that matter—as small towns. Nevertheless, the repetition of "Small Town" remains tolerable and the young man in "Rumbleseat" certainly is likable, as he reminds us of ourselves.

Mellencamp abhors aristocratic conceit and now pursues a chest-beating love of the democratic way, particularly as this lifestyle is defined in the Midwest. As all the rules seem to be changing—right in the middle of the game—Mellencamp's intentions make him the Tarzan of rock and roll, rather than the Peter Pan. This dedicated sincerity and raw moxie just might tickle the imagination of the buying public.

CHAPTER FIFTEEN

PARTING COMMENTS

For somebody who has never even met John Jay Mellencamp, I know a great deal about him—quite possibly more than anybody else who is not a close friend or relative.

Like all of us, John strives to establish his own identity, recognition, and independence. Growing up in Seymour, John depended upon his physical strength, rather than his scholastic talent or athletic poise, to create his image. Hence the result was the "bravado" image of the macho fighter, the reckless boozer, and the fornicating womanizer. Today, when he wears a sleeveless shirt, John still sports an impressive set of biceps, even though he is sometimes embarrassed by the stereotype that the media so often hypes—albeit with John's assistance. John has been inhibited by a fear of adulthood and a fixation on his teenage years. These hang-ups have created adjustment problems for the popular rocker, but as I have indicated, success has had a positive impact upon John, rather than a negative one.

Unlike most of us, however, John now finds himself wrestling with the inherent evils of the rock world and the growing demands of greatness. Ironically, John Mellencamp likes people, but this somewhat camera-shy personality has not yet learned how to handle all situations gracefully and diplomatically. He still suffers from the apparent inferiority complex that has been plaguing him for years. Accepting the challenge and the adventure of being a viable influence on the contemporary rock scene has convinced John to confront certain weaknesses. For example, he has eliminated booze and dope from his life. Now Marlboros are his only form of substance abuse. John has also accepted the role of father, making up for some lost time with his oldest daughter and not repeating the same mistake with his younger daughters. Success has forced him to realize that music and bands are not the *only* important aspects of life. Comfortable living and financial stability have allowed him to enjoy fathering. Being thirty-four, instead of nineteen, has also helped clarify his priorities. Like his parents, John experienced years of struggling. Like his parents, his perseverence paid dividends. Like his father, John can thank his wife Priscilla for her moral encouragement, her financial support, and her physical stamina. Like his mom and dad, John and Cil were a team. Even divorced, John and Cil remain friends.

Like most of us, John himself admires famous people. First, John's current favorite in the rock world is Prince. With the success of *Purple Rain,* as a movie and as an album, we see that Mellencamp is not alone in his appreciation of Prince. John also identifies with James Dean, another Hoosier, from Fairmount. An actor, Dean was killed in 1955, but John Jay Mellencamp tuned in to the legend. No doubt, our curent rocker saw himself in Dean's father-versus-son movies, like *Rebel without a Cause*. Dean's relationships with his film fathers were explosive, yet the boy constantly competed for recognition from his father. Unlike John, however, James Dean had no grandfather to turn to. John also admires the movies of Paul Newman, whose relative small size and impressive macho image strike home. In literature, John's fancy apparently turns to Tennessee Williams, the playwright who captured the steamy lust and the prisonlike confinement of small towns and dead-end blue-collar occupations. As could be expected, John Cougar Mellencamp sends contradictory signals to us in his "heroes" also. Both "macho strong" and "vulnerable androgenous" appeal to him. Either way, John shows himself to be a fan.

Like most stars, John has a strong sense of ego. He worries about overexposure, but forgets that many of the articles written about him have been for localized publications, such as newspapers and magazines in Seymour, Bloomington, or Indianapolis. By and large, the rest of the country has no access to these issues. Also, MTV and Cinemax remain unavailable in many areas of the country. Few of us own a satellite dish like John's. He also fields various opportunities. Something went askew with the plans for John to write the theme song for the soundtrack of Dustin Hoffman's *Tootsie*. John has, however, coauthored a song for the new Barbra Streisand album. The song is titled "You're a Step in the Right Direction." Plans also continue for his acting debut in a movie tentatively titled *Ridin' the Cage*. And as he grows older, he is developing his social conscience. He expressed empathy for the workers in Pittsburgh, as they were holding elections when he was there in the spring of 1984. He will undoubtedly be lending his support (and his recognizable image) to various functions. Fans should keep their eyes pealed for this inevitable change: the irresponsible, overly indulgent kid will grow up and become an adult, aware individual. Nuclear war, for example, worries all of us, including John Mellencamp. In another area, rock personalities are encouraging young people to "feel the power" by registering to vote. Perhaps these stars will eventually endorse other political issues, like nuclear disarmament, unemployment, and educational achievement. Even though some rockers—like John himself—have negated the idea that they have an impact upon their young fans, that impact does exist. As John's hot temperament simmers into a cooler, even-tempered establishment figure, he'll be asked to participate in such ventures. The Farm Aid concert is one small example, reflecting a reborn awareness and a sincere concern.

In the past, John has not endeared himself to many. Is this why his videos didn't receive more accolades during the *MTV Video Award* show that aired in September 1984. "Authority Song" lost in the category of Best Cinematography. When Mark Goodman, the MTV video jockey, spoke to John in the "heavy jewelry" section of the audience, an unshaven John charmingly said he was pleased to have such good seats. He was only four or five rows back, but I wonder *why* he was passed over. He did not seem concerned about not being nominated, though. Much has already been written about the "incestlike" selection procedure of the nominated videos on the MTV awards show, yet why was "Pink Houses" not recognized? This fine video was released during the time period covered by the award show, but for some reason, the video wasn't recognized.

Those who know John or work for him hesitate to criticize him or say anything negative about him. The loyalty is admirable and necessary—though a bit contrived sometimes. One person, a former employer of a younger John Mellencamp, asked me if I had ever met John. When I said I had not, she said that when I did, I would probably not like him, because he frequently makes a poor first impression. One has to grow accustomed to John; as with fine wine, I guess, age sweetens the initial reaction. I figured I would not find him abrasive, since I felt I had a pretty accurate idea of what makes John tick. A Poly Gram promoter invited one girl I know backstage at a concert in Chicago, but she (not a Cougar fan) found John to be the epitome of conceit. Of course, backstage after a performance is probably a poor time to meet such a star. After all, he is working, tired, and dealing with many problems.

John is learning a great deal, as he completes his initiation rite of passage into stardom. Success has improved John's working relationships with his family: instead of affection, a guarded respect between father and son; a reconciliatory friendliness with Priscilla; and a part-time source of employment, when on tour, for his brother Ted and his cousin Tracy. Success has also enhanced John's working relationship with the recording personnel and the media folks. But fans cannot help but laugh at the inherent irony of somebody like John Cougar taking somebody else to task for being arrogant and condescending! Success has also provided John with the inner peace and the outer confidence to explore new dimensions to his career. No longer trying to run the devil bowlegged or to shock those around him with profanity, he is working with Zalman King on a motion picture. Could this be the same Zalman King who starred in a 1971 flick called *The Ski Bum?* This movie was filmed in Vail, Colorado, and King portrayed an antiestablishment adolescent at a ski resort. Move the setting to Indiana and make the skis a motorcycle and whom do we have? I hope that *Ridin' the Cage,* John's movie, is superior to *The Ski Bum.* If Larry McMurty, who wrote *Hud* and *Terms of Endearment,* has actually edited the screenplay John himself wrote, Warner Brothers probably will have a quality movie. John candidly admitted that his own version needed drastic help, yet he still feels proud about dealing with the impact the downward economy has had on guys his age.

John is becoming big-time, whether or not he cares to admit it. In September of 1976, after the release of *Chestnut Street Incident,* John became associated with the small band scene in Bloomington. Such bands as the Gizmos and MX-80 Sound recorded on the Gulcher label. On the Gulcher label, John himself recorded at least one seven-inch record with four cuts. Called *U.S. Male,* the record contains four songs: "Kicks," "2,000 A.D.," "Lou-Ser," and "Hot Man." A picture sleeve shows Cougar standing in front of two mailboxes, but the *U.S. Male* title is supposed to refer to the many concerns a young man had at that time: the environment, decadence, employment, manliness, and money. John's teen years, remember, were the turbulent sixties.

This recording artist from the Gulcher label has proven his critics wrong. Thus far he has remained in the Seymour/Bloomington area, but should he become a serious actor, or a producer or promoter, or an even more potent force in the world of rock singers and songwriters, relocating in New York or Los Angeles might become necessary. Hopefully, he will remain in the Hoosier heartland, yet as other aspects of his image mature, he cannot allow his past to imperil his future. Again, Time, with her perpetual ticktock, will unveil the reality. But those who see John Mellencamp as nothing more than a substance-abusing, flaming fool, with little or no real talent, are being forced to confront the talent, charisma, and determination of this spiritual rocker.

Just who is this boy/man known to us as John Cougar Mellencamp? Is he a jerk or a genius? Only an idiot would deny that John has certainly committed some incredibly shortsighted and highly irresponsible acts. Yet even his harshest critics must not blind themselves to the turnabout that success, maturity, and credibility have initiated. John is projecting a boyish charm, a direct sincerity, and a keen talent. Maybe this is genius: to possess the wisdom to admit to one's errors, harness the courage to redefine one's priorities, and strengthen the position one holds in the occupational field he or she loves. Nevertheless, all of the doubters can "eat crow." The kid who broke all the rules and did everything wrong is no jerk. God must be smiling upon him, which makes me happy. John Jay Mellencamp appeals to our communal heartstrings and makes us feel positive about ourselves by laughing at ourselves.

Of course, being a successful rock star who is becoming a millionaire makes a person different from the rest of us who are not in the public spotlight. A chuckle also rumbles within me whenever I hear some famous person claim that whirlwind success has not changed him. He is still the "boy next door." How ignorant do they assume we are? Their sense of honesty would freeze beer! True, I have never met John Mellencamp. But I won't believe that the acclaim and recognition that he has encountered over the past two or three years have left him unchanged. Believing this would require him to be a humanoid or something. Trying to remain a symbol of what authentic rock and roll is supposed to be is fine. On the other hand, we tend to spend and to invest the cash that we make. This conspicuous-consumption syndrome has already bitten John, to some extent. Money will force him to "sell out" this symbolic refuge. He may well feel badly about it, but this emergence into the big time will impose other changes, without automatically destroying him.

Nevertheless, John's rejection of the rock and roll trick bag is admirable. Saying that he is one of thousands of guys who have had hit records is true. But those thousands, in numbers, will pale at the realization of the thousands upon thousands who fail to produce a hit record. Don't berate your accomplishment, John. Realize that egotism is not necessarily a curse. Realize, also, that your position of grandeur will necessitate your talking down to people, will require you to be the heavy, and will require you to alter your deportment. Remember all the trivial duties you had to do yourself, but now you hire people to do them. Notice the slight bulge of blubber in the stomach area, the symbol of affluence. This is what success and wealth are all about: a reminder to each of us that populist thinking and the American dream travel in harmony. Appreciate what you have and continue to walk that fine line between TCB (taking care of business) and taking yourself *too* seriously.

Steve Wynn, of the Dream Syndicate, spoke recently about John's contribution to the recent scene of rock and roll: "I think John Cougar is the best spokesman of our time. The guy's not fucking around. He says, 'Well, I'm an idiot, but I know what I like, and where I come from, people want to hear rock 'n' roll.' John Cougar's a better spokesman for our time than any art critic's band. I mean, what has Gang of Four done for the heartlands of America that John Cougar hasn't done?"[1] Steve Wynn is toasting a star whose work he admires. This book, I hope, has done likewise. Looking at a performing artist—studying both his life and his work—is an overwhelming responsibility.

John sometimes says that he hasn't changed; all that is different is the public's perception of him. Obviously, I take issue with this. John Jay Mellencamp has to be different from what he was three or four years ago. Contrary to what he says, he is not doing "the same old shit" he has always done. As a wealthy person, he needs to stop asserting that the money means nothing and that he is bored with John Cougar. Maybe he is growing weary of the Cougar image, but the money and the success that generated it have allowed John Mellencamp to relax, become a successful provider, learn to love fatherhood, and continue laughing at himself. As long as John Cougar Mellencamp can laugh at himself, we have hope that we can laugh at ourselves. This laughter helps us feel comfortable with ourselves and with our own realtity. Please let the laughter live on!

NOTES

Chapter 2. Romanticism versus Naturalism

1. Lisa Robinson, "The John Cougar Mellencamp Interview," *Rock Video*, June 1984, p. 60.
2. "John Cougar Mellencamp: Sex, Violence and Rock 'n' Roll," *Rock Fever*, May 1984, p. 74.

Chapter 3. Coming of Age

1. "John Cougar Mellencamp: Sex, Violence and Rock 'n' Roll," *Rock Fever*, May 1984, p. 59.
2. Ibid.
3. Ibid.
4. Lisa Robinson, "The John Cougar Mellencamp Interview," *Rock Video*, June 1984, p. 60.
5. "John Cougar Mellencamp: Open File," *Rock Fever*, July 1984, p. 14.
6. Ibid., p. 15.
7. Robinson, "John Cougar Mellencamp Interview," p. 66.
8. Ibid.
9. Christopher Connelly, "Hey, John Cougar, What's Your Problem?," *Rolling Stone*, December 9, 1982, p. 24.
10. Ibid.
11. Bill Holdship, "John Cougar, Rock 'Star'? Pink Houses in the Midwest," *Creem*, January 1984, p. 33.
12. Robinson, "John Cougar Mellencamp Interview," p. 66.

13. "John Cougar Mellencamp: In His Own Words," *Hit Parader,* Fall 1984, p. 55.
14. Holdship, "John Cougar, Rock 'Star'?," p. 35.
15. Robinson, "John Cougar Mellencamp Interview," p. 60.
16. "John Cougar Mellencamp: Open File," p. 14.
17. "John Cougar Mellencamp: In His Own Words," p. 55.
18. "John Cougar Mellencamp: Sex, Violence and Rock 'n' Roll," p. 59.
19. Ibid.
20. "John Cougar Mellencamp: In His Own Words," p. 55.
21. Ibid.
22. Holdship, "John Cougar, Rock 'Star'?," p. 35.
23. Connelly, "Hey, John Cougar," p. 23.
24. Ibid.
25. "John Cougar Mellencamp: Open File," p. 15.
26. Holdship, "John Cougar, Rock 'Star'?," p. 35.
27. Ibid., p. 34.
28. "John Cougar Mellencamp: In His Own Words," p. 55.
29. Mikael Kirke, "John Cougar Mellencamp: Back Home in Indiana, the Cougar Turns Pussycat—Well, Almost," *Faces,* February 1984, p. 23.

Chapter 4. Sweet Success

1. Bill Holdship, "John Cougar, Rock 'Star'? Pink Houses in the Midwest," *Creem,* January 1984, p. 31.
2. Lisa Robinson, "John Cougar Mellencamp Interview," *Rock Video,* June 1984, p. 59.
3. Ibid., p. 60.
4. "John Cougar Mellencamp: In His Own Words," *Hit Parader,* Fall 1984, p. 55.
5. Holdship, "John Cougar, Rock 'Star'?," p. 33.
6. Robinson, "John Cougar Mellencamp Interview," p. 61.
7. Ibid.
8. Mikael Kirke, "John Cougar Mellencamp: Back Home in Indiana, the Cougar Turns Pussycat—Well, Almost," *Faces,* February 1984, p. 20.

9. Robinson, "John Cougar Mellencamp Interview," p. 66.
10. Holdship, "John Cougar, Rock 'Star'?," p. 33.
11. "John Cougar Mellencamp: In His Own Words," p. 55.
12. "John Cougar Mellencamp: Sex, Violence and Rock 'n' Roll," *Rock Fever*, May 1984, p. 74.
13. Holdship, "John Cougar, Rock 'Star'?," pp. 34–35.
14. Ibid., p. 34.
15. Ibid., p. 35.
16. "John Cougar Mellencamp: Open File," *Rock Fever*, July 1984, p. 15.
17. Holdship, "John Cougar, Rock 'Star'?," p. 35.
18. Kirke, "John Cougar Mellencamp: Back Home in Indiana," p. 23.
19. Ibid.
20. Ibid.

Chapter 5. The Guy I Hate

1. Jim Plump, "John Cougar: Six Million To One," *The Maple Tree*, 1982, p. 8.
2. Lynn Van Matre, "Cougar Comes to Grips with His Success," *Indianapolis Star*, August 22, 1982, p. 6E.
3. Ibid., p. 1E.
4. Bill Holdship, "John Cougar, Rock 'Star'? Pink Houses in the Midwest," *Creem*, January 1984, p. 34.
5. Christopher Connelly, "Hey, John Cougar, What's Your Problem?," *Rolling Stone*, December 9, 1982, p. 23.
6. Jill Warren, "Night Life: John Cougar a Rock 'n' Roll 'Bad Boy'?," *Indianapolis Star*, October 15, 1982, p. 34.
7. Ibid.
8. Giovanna Breu, "Neither John Mellencamp nor His Rock Persona, John Cougar, Is an American Fool," *People*, October 11, 1982, p. 128.
9. Holdship, "John Cougar, Rock 'Star'?," p. 34.
10. Ibid.
11. Harry Knight, telephone interview, Saturday, August 18, 1984.

12. Brantley Blythe, personal interview, Saturday, August 18, 1984.
13. Breu, "Neither John Mellencamp nor His Rock Persona, John Cougar, Is an American Fool," p. 128 and 133.
14. Brantley Blythe, quoted in Ross Allen, "At the Top of the Rock: Cougar Country," *Indianapolis Magazine*, April 1983, p. 29.
15. Ibid.
16. Plump, "John Cougar," p. 7.
17. Ross Allen, "At the Top of the Rock: Cougar Country," *Indianapolis Magazine*, April 1983, p. 30.
18. Van Matre, "Cougar Comes to Grips with His Success," p. 6E.
19. Allen, "Top of the Rock," p. 28.
20. Ibid.
21. Mrs. Patty Crane, personal interview, Saturday, August 18, 1984.
22. Connelly, "Hey, John Cougar," p. 24.
23. Ritchie Clark, personal interview, Saturday, August 18, 1984.

Chapter 6. Son of Seymour

1. Mrs. Patty Crane, personal interview, Saturday, August 18, 1984.
2. Mayor William W. Bailey, personal letter, Tuesday, September 4, 1984.
3. Officer Richard Pennybaker, telephone interview, Tuesday, August 28, 1984.

Chapter 8. *The Kid Inside*

1. Bill Holdship, "John Cougar, Rock 'Star'? Pink Houses in the Midwest," *Creem*, January 1984, p. 35.
2. Andrew Slater, "John Cougar Finds an Answer for his Critics," *Rolling Stone*, September 16, 1982, p. 43.
3. "John Cougar Mellencamp: Open File," *Rock Fever*, July 1984, pp. 14–15.

Chapter 11. *Nothing Matters and What if It Did?*

1. Andrew Slater, "John Cougar Finds an Answer for his Critics," *Rolling Stone*, September 16, 1982, p. 43.

Chapter 15. *Parting Comments*

1. Bill Holdship, "John Cougar, Rock 'Star'? Pink Houses in the Midwest," *Creem*, January 1984, p. 33.

BIBLIOGRAPHY

The author apologizes for incomplete bibliographic data. Friends and fans offered copies of the articles they are collecting in scrapbooks, but they did not recall the original source of the information.

Allen, Ross, "At the Top of the Rock: Cougar Country." *Indianapolis Magazine* 20, April 1983.
Bailey, William W. Personal correspondence to author. September 4, 1984.
Blythe, Brantley. Interview with the author. August 18, 1984.
Breu, Giovanna, "Neither John Mellencamp Nor His Rock Personna, John Cougar, Is An American Fool," *People* 18, October 11, 1982.
Clark, Ritchie. Interview with the author. August 18, 1984.
Connelly, Christopher, "Hey, John Cougar, What's Your Problem?," *Rolling Stone*, December 9, 1982.
Crane, Patty. Interview with the author. August 18, 1984.
Farris, Judy. Interview with the author. August 20, 1984.
Holdship, Bill. "John Cougar, Rock 'Star'? Pink Houses in the Midwest." *Creem* 15, January 1984.
"John Cougar Mellencamp: Coulda Been a Contender!" *Creem Rock-Shots*, July 1984.
"John Cougar Mellencamp: In His Own Words." *Hit Parader*, Fall 1984.
"John Cougar Mellencamp: Open File." *Rock Fever* 1, July 1984.
"John Cougar Mellencamp: Sex, Violence and Rock 'n' Roll." *Rock Fever 1*, May 1984.

Kirke, Mikael. "John Cougar Mellencamp: Back Home in Indiana, the Cougar Turns Pussycat—Well, Almost." *Faces 1*, February 1984.

Knight, Harry. Telephone interview with the author. August 18, 1984.

Mellencamp, Laura. Interview with the author. August 21, 1984.

Pennybaker, Richard. Telephone interview with the author. August 28, 1984.

Pille, Jacques. "John Cougar: Street-wise Rocker Matures."

Plump, Jim. "John Cougar: Six Million to One." *The Maple Tree*, 1982.

Riegel, Richard. "John Cougar: X-R 7's Entire Midwest Metropolis." *Creem 12*, December, 1980.

Robinson, Lisa. "The John Cougar Mellencamp Interview." *Rock Video*, June 1894.

Slater, Andrew. "John Cougar Finds an Answer for his Critics." *Rolling Stone*, September 16, 1982.

"Uh-Huh! John 'Cougar' Mellencamp's Tribute to the Rolling Stones." *Video Rock Stars*, Spring 1984.

Van Matre, Lynn. "Cougar Comes to Grips with Success." *Indianapolis Star*, August 22, 1982.

Warren, Jill. "Night Life: John Cougar a Rock 'n' Roll 'Bad Boy'?" *Indianapolis Star*. October 15, 1982.